As one of the world's longest established
and best-known travel brands,
Thomas Cook are the experts in travel.

35 years our
the secrets
d the world,
a wealth of
on for travel.

Cook as your
your next trip
and benefit from our unique heritage.

Thomas Cook **pocket** guides

MONTE CARLO
Paul Medbourne

Written by Paul Medbourne, updated by Nick Inman & Clara Villanueva
Original photography and research by Ethel Davies

Published by Thomas Cook Publishing
A division of Thomas Cook Tour Operations Limited
Company registration no. 3772199 England
The Thomas Cook Business Park, 9 Coningsby Road,
Peterborough PE3 8SB, United Kingdom
Email: books@thomascook.com, Tel: +44 (0) 1733 416477
www.thomascookpublishing.com

Produced by Cambridge Publishing Management Limited
Burr Elm Court, Main Street, Caldecote CB23 7NU
www.cambridgepm.co.uk

ISBN: 978-1-84848-504-4

© 2006, 2008, 2009 Thomas Cook Publishing
This fourth edition © 2011 Thomas Cook Publishing
Text © Thomas Cook Publishing
Maps © Thomas Cook Publishing/PCGraphics (UK) Limited
Transport map © Communicarta Limited

Series Editor: Karen Beaulah
Production/DTP: Steven Collins

Printed and bound in Spain by GraphyCems

Cover photography © George Contorakes/Masterfile

CONTENTS

SYMBOLS KEY

The following symbols are used throughout this book:

ⓐ address ⓣ telephone ⓦ website address ⓛ opening times
ⓝ public transport connections ⓘ important

The following symbols are used on the maps:

𝑖	information office	◼	point of interest
✈	airport	◯	city
✚	hospital	◯	large town
🛡	police station	○	small town
▤	railway station	═	motorway
✝	cathedral	―	main road
❶	numbers denote	―	minor road
	featured cafés & restaurants	―	railway
		---	international border

Hotels and restaurants are graded by approximate price as follows:
£ budget price **££** mid-range price **£££** expensive

Abbreviations used in addresses:

av	avenue
blvd	boulevard
espl	esplanade
pl	place (square)
prom	promenade
sq	square

▶ *Flashy yachts adorn the harbour*

INTRODUCING
Monte Carlo & Monaco

Introduction

Perched precipitously between the Mediterranean and the mountains of the Alpes-Maritimes, Monaco is the second-smallest independent state on earth (after the Vatican City), with a surface area of just 2 sq km (less than 1 sq mile) – yet it is known the world over. The name never fails to conjure up ideas of millionaires and tax havens, celebrities and fashion, luxury yachts, Grand Prix racing and, of course, the world's most famous casino in Monte Carlo.

Budgeteers will be pleased to hear that, despite all the glitz, Monaco has plenty of sights and attractions to offer non-millionaires – not to mention a superb climate and a handy proximity to Italy and the Côte d'Azur. Visually, it is stunning: every park is a jewel of manicured perfection, with flowers lovingly tended by the veritable army of gardeners that Monaco employs. Its architecture is remarkably bold: Monaco has a reputation for experimenting with brave new styles – a quality that prompted a world architectural expert to comment that 'every great architectural success and mistake made in the past century is represented in Monaco'.

The Principality of Monaco, itself barely the size of a small village, is divided into several distinct quarters, of which Monte Carlo is the best known. The official language is French but in practice Monaco is trilingual in French, English and Italian. The Monégasque people (as the locals are known) over the centuries found themselves propelled on to a global stage by the visions of their enterprising monarchs, and now it is estimated that native Monégasques make up only 7,000 of the 35,000 population.

Since the incredibly brazen capture of Monaco by the first Grimaldi (see page 14), little has changed in the ambitious spirit of the royal family. Monaco's face is constantly changing. In recent years, it has seen the arrival of the Grimaldi Forum, a huge and mostly underground conference and leisure centre; the Monte Carlo Bay Hotel, the largest and most ambitious in Monaco's history; the Digue, a floating pier; and Fontvieille, an entire district built on land reclaimed from the sea. Monaco showcases a steady stream of exciting events and exhibitions, and prides itself on championing new creative talent. Monaco has the money, the looks and the fame, but for many its ambitious and innovative spirit is its true wealth.

🔺 *Monaco's lavish Mediterranean waterfront*

When to go

The emergence of no-frills airlines has made Monaco much more accessible for short breaks. However, the seasonal fare variations can be staggering: a week's return trip on a low-cost airline from a London airport in July will cost around 30 per cent less than the same journey in August, and early spring can cost a tenth of peak summer. It pays to investigate thoroughly before choosing dates.

Seasonality affects accommodation prices, too. The high season is late July–late August. In the shoulder season, from early April to mid-July and September, rates can be 30–50 per cent lower; if you fancy a late autumn, winter or early spring break you may find hotels offering a further reduction of 10–20 per cent on the mid-season prices. Special accommodation packages in these months offer particularly good value.

SEASONS & CLIMATE

The earliest tourists on the Riviera, mainly wealthy British, came in the 18th and 19th centuries in search of winter warmth. Monaco averages 300 days of sunshine per year, and in winter the daytime temperature stays in the range 8–14°C (48–58°F), with sunny days and cool nights. Spring brings the strong wind of *le mistral* but slightly warmer days, and in summer the temperatures can reach 27°C (80°F), though mitigated by sea breezes, especially in the evening. From the weather point of view September and October are definitely the best months in which to visit – temperatures are a comfortable 15–21°C (60–70°F) and it's still possible to get a tan in October.

ANNUAL EVENTS

Monaco's events calendar isn't only about motor racing, despite the popular assumption. Its concerts, whether classical, jazz or pop,

MONTE CARLO RALLY

The most famous annual event organised by the Automobile Club de Monaco is of course the Grand Prix (see page 12), which always coincides with Ascension Day in May and has taken place 70 times since its inauguration in 1929. Its older cousin, scarcely less famous, is the Monte Carlo Rally at the end of January. The Rally started in 1911 when Monaco's authorities, concerned by the dip in tourism and casino revenues caused by the carnival's revival in nearby Nice, planned an event that would bring the punters back to Monte Carlo and demonstrate just how delightful the climate could be in January. Participants came from all over Europe to take part in the inaugural rally, and they still do to this day. The number of entrants is now limited to 60 and, as the event forms parts of the FIA World Championship, it's a serious competition. Drivers set off from Monte Carlo for three separate legs of the competition on three consecutive days, covering over 100 km (60 miles) each day on circular courses which run through the nearby mountains. ☎ 93 15 26 00 Ⓦ www.acm.mc

always showcase the current top global performers, and its ballet, opera and circus acts are world-class. If any play is proving a hit in Paris, you can bet that Monaco's cultural authorities will be busy working behind the scenes to bring the show to the Principality. For a comprehensive calendar of what's on, check out the tourist authority website Ⓦ www.visitmonaco.com. You can also pick up the monthly booklet *Bienvenue* (see page 153) for information on upcoming events and festivals.

January

St Dévote's Day Monaco celebrates its patron saint Ste Dévote on 27 January. On the eve of the festival a small boat arrives at the port and is taken in procession and placed outside the church dedicated to the saint. After the arrival of the Prince's family, there is a religious ceremony and the boat is set alight, followed by fireworks. Local children then scour its burnt-out wreckage for nails, said to bring good luck for the coming year.

June

Feast of St John the Baptist The evening of 23 June sees folk groups from all over the Mediterranean gather to perform traditional music and dance alongside Monaco's own ensemble, the Palladienne, in Place du Palais. The Prince attends a service in the Palace chapel and then two liveried footmen light a bonfire. The next day a procession forms in Place des Moulins in Monte Carlo and marches to the parish church, St-Charles. After a service the crowd dances the rest of the day and night away in a great open-air ball.

July

Sciaratù The tradition of having a good time just before the rigours of Lent is as old in Monaco as in nearby Nice, but in Monaco the event lapsed until about 30 years ago, when it was revived under the local dialect name *Sciaratù* and moved to the summer. Much like the Nice Carnival, it is marked by processions, dummy heads, confetti battles and open-air dancing.

August

Festival of St-Romain A chapel was built in the 16th century to this martyred Roman legionary in the hamlet of Les Moulins, but the festivities now take place every 9 August in Monaco-Ville's Jardins St-Martin, with plenty of open-air dancing and a lot of refreshments.

November
Monégasque National Holiday This holiday is celebrated on 19 November, the feast of St Rainier. The daytime is marked by a special mass, after which the reigning prince distributes honours and decorations. Night-time sees a gala evening at the Opéra and a firework display over the harbour.

PUBLIC HOLIDAYS
New Year's Day 1 Jan
St Dévote's Day 27 Jan
Easter Monday 9 Apr 2012, 1 Apr 2013, 21 Apr 2014
Labour Day 1 May
Ascension Day 17 May 2012, 9 May 2013, 29 May 2014
Whit Monday 28 May 2012, 19 May 2013, 9 June 2014
Corpus Christi 07 Jun 2012, 3 Jun 2013, 3 June 2014
Assumption of the Blessed Virgin Mary 15 Aug
All Saints' Day 1 Nov
National Day 19 Nov
Immaculate Conception 8 Dec
Christmas Day 25 Dec

On public holidays, public transport runs to Sunday schedules, and banks, post offices and public buildings are closed. Many shops (but not generally restaurants) will also be closed.

The Monaco Grand Prix

Few events in the Formula 1 Grand Prix season have quite the same excitement as the Monaco Grand Prix: this was the first F1 street race, and is one of the season's most difficult courses. Millions who have never visited Monaco are familiar with the layout of the city centre through broadcasts of this historic race.

In 1925, the Monaco Cycling Club decided to rename itself the Automobile Club de Monaco, and applied to become a member of the International Association of Recognised Automobile Clubs; it was turned down on the grounds that Monaco organised no motorsport events on its own territory. Stung to the quick, the Monégasques set about removing all the obstacles, physical and organisational, to holding a race through their streets. On 14 April 1929, Prince Pierre inaugurated the 1st Monaco Grand Prix with a lap of honour in a Torpedo Voisin. The 16-car race that followed was won by a Bugatti driven by William Grover-Williams, an Englishman who had arrived too late to take part in the official trial sessions. The average speed over the 100 laps was just 80 kph (50 mph)!

Today, the course is much the same as the original one, though modifications take place from time to time (notably, in 1976, the addition of the famous Rascasse hairpin bend); its 3.3 km (2 miles) are now raced over 78 laps by more than 20 cars. The Monaco Grand Prix takes place every year in late May, the programme extending from Thursday to Sunday. Normal traffic is barred from the course during these days. Practice runs take place on the Thursday and on Saturday morning, while Saturday afternoon sees the F1 qualifying session. The race begins at 14.00 (local time) on Sunday.

Tickets for seats to watch the race cost from €305 to €550 and are available in advance from the Automobile Club de Monaco.

Some restaurants offer lunch menus for tables on their terraces overlooking the circuit. Residents with a view of the course make a small fortune renting out their balconies. Hotel rooms during the race period are very difficult to find, as so many are block-booked annually; better to stay in Menton or even Nice and travel in for the event.

The upcoming dates are: 24–27 May 2012, 23–26 May 2013, 26–29 May 2014. **Automobile Club de Monaco** Ⓐ 23 blvd Albert 1er, Monte Carlo ⓣ 93 15 26 00 Ⓦ www.acm.mc and www.grand-prix-monaco.com

⬤ *Monaco can claim to have the most luxurious trackside seats of any F1 event*

History

Unlike many sovereign states, Monaco can trace its beginnings very precisely to the date of 8 January 1297. Up till then this area of the Italian coast had been a battleground for the two major factions of medieval Italy, the Guelphs (supporters of the pope) and the Ghibellines (the league of cities and families backing the holy Roman emperor. The Ghibellines had built a castle in 1215 on the site of what is now Monaco's palace, but on that fateful night in 1297, François Grimaldi, a Guelph from Genoa, tricked his way in by disguising his followers as monks, and seized the fortress. François and his successors established themselves as rulers.

By 1489 the two major powers in the area, France and Savoy, were ready to formally acknowledge Monaco's independence. In 1612 the reigning Grimaldi, Honoré II, gave himself the title of Prince of Monaco, and the Principality came into being; he later signed a treaty which effectively tied his country's foreign policy to that of France for good, while reaffirming Monaco's sovereignty. The only interruption to this relationship came with the French Revolution, when the Grimaldis were temporarily dispossessed, but normality was restored in 1814 with the overthrow of Napoleon.

The next big change came in 1861, when Charles III realised he needed new sources of revenue. His answer was to found the Casino on the Plateau des Spélugues, renamed Monte Carlo (Charles' Hill), in 1866. With the advent of the railway, bringing wealthy gamblers and tourists from all over Europe, the Principality's fortunes took a steady upswing. Charles' second masterstroke was to exempt residents from most taxes, ensuring the stream of tax exiles from whom Monaco has benefited ever since.

The early 20th century saw the reign of Albert I, who sponsored the Oceanographic Institute, scientific expeditions to South America and many other technological advances. In 1949 Prince Rainier III came to the throne and caught the world's attention by marrying film star Grace Kelly; Princess Grace's death following a motor accident in 1982 was a tragedy shared by the whole world. Although the behaviour of some of the princely family often attracted unwelcome publicity, Rainier himself remained popular until the end of his long reign, dying in 2005 to be succeeded by his son Albert II, the current prince. In July 2011 Albert married South African Olympic swimmer Charlene Wittstock. Since his accession he has acquired a reputation for encouraging entrepreneurial spirit and environmental responsibility, both within the Principality and around the world. He has created a foundation to protect the environment and to encourage sustainable development.

○ The Palais Princier, residence of the prince, dates from the 12th century

Lifestyle

When Charles III opened the Casino and its associated hotels in 1866 (see page 14), he ushered in the world's first state that was devoted entirely to pleasure – for visitors, that is. Pleasure then meant gambling, shopping, drinking and fine dining, and the clientele was Europe's elite (give or take a few penniless adventurers and con men). It was quickly denounced in other parts of the world as a hell on earth given over to every kind of vice, and with publicity like that it couldn't fail. Today the visitor profile is more democratic, and there are many more cultural and fun attractions than gambling away your inheritance or what scandalised Victorian commentators called 'acts of gallantry' (roughly anything that involved men and women taking their clothes off).

The other side of the picture is less evident to the casual visitor: the 7,000 or so native Monégasque citizens (less than a quarter of the country's population) are a conservative lot, whose pleasures are more likely to be found in traditional saint's day celebrations (see page 10) or quiet family occasions. Apparently untroubled by political or economic issues (they didn't see the need for a national constitution until 1911, for instance), they get on with their lives in an atmosphere of respectability and devotion to the ruling family. By law they can't even enter casinos except to work there.

This is not to say that they are unfriendly, inhospitable or intolerant of their visitors; however, they do take pains to preserve Monaco's image as an upmarket playground. The most obvious symptom of this is the public dress code. Though topless bathing is fine on the beach, appearing anywhere else in Monaco bare-chested, barefoot or wearing swimsuits will soon invite the attention of the police. It also pays to defer to some of the formal courtesy that the Monégasques, like the French, observe. Don't forget to greet the shopkeeper with *bonjour* (hello) and say *au revoir* (goodbye) when you leave; include a *s'il vous plaît* (please) when you ask for something and a *merci* (thank you) when you receive it. Call the waiter *monsieur* and the waitress *madame*. Unless you are addressed in English first, it is polite to begin a conversation or request with a local in a few words of your best French, if only to establish that you are a civilised visitor and to acknowledge that you are a guest in someone else's country.

⬥ *Luxury motors are all part of Monte Carlo's glamorous lifestyle*

Culture

Monaco's wealth enables it to put on a programme of events in the arts, theatre, opera, ballet and music that is rivalled by only a few of the world's cities. Add to that one or two internationally acclaimed museums, and it is easy to see why this tiny country attracts so many culture vultures.

Since its creation in 1879, the **Opéra de Monte-Carlo** (ⓐ Pl du Casino ⓣ 98 06 28 00 ⓦ www.opera.mc) has gained international fame, playing a key role in promoting its singers' beautiful voices to the rest of Europe. It maintains a reputation for artistic innovation. Historically, composers of the calibre of Bizet, Franck and Massenet chose the Opéra de Monte Carlo to début their works. Today, it maintains a classical repertoire mixed with more modern newcomers. Performances are held not only in the original Salle Garnier of the Casino (see page 64), but also in newer venues such as the Grimaldi Forum (see page 65) and the Espace Fontvieille (see page 103).

Les Ballets de Monte-Carlo (ⓣ 92 16 24 20 ⓦ www.balletsde montecarlo.com) started as a dance academy founded by Princess Grace and was restructured in 1985 under choreographer Jean-Christophe Maillot. It is now reviving the Principality's formerly strong tradition in ballet.

The **Monte Carlo Philharmonic Orchestra** (ⓐ Auditorium Rainier III, Blvd Louis II ⓣ 93 10 85 00 ⓦ www.opmc.mc) was first established in 1863. Many great conductors of the 20th century, from Arturo Toscanini to Leonard Bernstein and Lorin Maazel, have led the orchestra in concert.

To find out what's on during your stay and book tickets for performing arts spectacles, drop in at the tourist office.

● *Les Ballets de Monte-Carlo*

The most visible evidence of the Grimaldis' commitment to the visual arts is the astonishing Chemins des Sculptures, which decorates the whole length of Monaco before coming to a grand climax in the Parc Paysager de Fontvieille (see page 103). Monaco has always attracted artists, and today there are many temporary art exhibitions on themes as diverse as Latin American sculpture to 'Dali at Monte Carlo'. For a more permanent exhibition, the Marlborough Gallery (see page 92) is the place to view the output of Monaco's contemporary crop of artists.

Although a number of Monaco's museums are more visitor attractions than cultural centres, at least two are world leaders in the study of their subjects. The Oceanographic Institute (see page 84), founded in the early 20th century by the scientifically minded Prince Albert I, is at the forefront of oceanic research, and its excellent museum should be visited by anyone with even the slightest interest in marine wildlife and conservation. Its botanical equivalent is the Jardin Exotique (see page 90), where the dry-climate plants of the world are grown, studied and propagated; the terraced garden of cacti and other succulents is fascinating at any time of the year. Although the subject may appear trivial in comparison, the collection of dolls and moving figures lovingly assembled by Mme Madeleine Galéa and bequeathed to the Nouveau Musée National de Monaco (page 66) is a delight. Those with more of a need for speed will find plenty to interest them in Prince Rainier's collection of 20th-century automobiles at the Collection des Voitures Anciennes in Fontvieille (see page 105).

▶ *Place du Casino is the very heart of Monte Carlo*

MAKING THE MOST OF
Monte Carlo & Monaco

Shopping

It has to be said that Monaco is not the place for bargains. Not surprisingly, given the presence of so many millionaires in its population, every famous designer name has an establishment here, along with a lot of upmarket local specialists. Exclusive clothes come with exclusive price tags. Bear this in mind if venturing into Ventimiglia market where the goods are only cheaper because they're fake (see page 130).

If your credit card will stand it, or if you are an untiring window-shopper, there is a wealth of boutiques to keep you entertained in Monaco. There are also markets and plenty of hypermarkets and humbler shops, especially in La Condamine and the Centre Commercial de Fontvieille , where you can acquire the foodstuffs and goods that attract foreign shoppers to France.

Whatever your retail needs, high-flying or mundane, you'll find the booklet *Monaco Shopping* invaluable; obtainable from the tourist office, this annual publication lists everything from dry cleaners to antiques emporia, hairdressers to high-class jewellers.

La Condamine is the best area for mainstream shopping. This is where you'll find the main food and flower market and the pedestrianised Rue Princesse Caroline shopping centre. Being near the yacht harbour of Port Hercule it also has a host of shops specialising in marine paraphernalia. It's the best place in town to look for genuine regional produce, and has the Principality's main quota of useful everyday shops – small supermarkets, pharmacies and the like. The more upmarket streets of Monte Carlo don't exactly lack butchers and bakers, but you may not notice them among the top-name designer outlets, the jewellers and couturiers. The Centre Commercial Le Métropole, at the hotel of the same

◖ *Boulevard des Moulins, one of the most fashionable shopping streets*

USEFUL SHOPPING PHRASES

What time do the shops open/close?
A quelle heure ouvrent/ferment les magasins?
Ah kehlur oovr/fehrm lay mahgazan?

How much is this?
C'est combien?
Cey combyahn?

Can I try this on?
Puis-je essayer ceci?
Pweezh ehsayay suhsee?

My size is ...
Ma taille (clothes)/ma pointure (shoes) est ...
Mah tie/mah pwantewr ay ...

I'll take this one, thank you
Je prends celui-ci/celle-ci, merci
Zhuhr prohng surlweesee/sehlsee, mehrsee

name (see page 39) facing the Casino gardens, alone has 80 shops, as well as cafés and restaurants for refreshment. However, the further north you stroll along Monte Carlo's boulevards, the more varied the shops become. Residential Fontvieille has its own, more down-to-earth Centre Commercial de Fontvieille, which includes a Carrefour hypermarket for food and general goods (a great place to pick up the contents of a picnic). In the narrow streets of Monaco-Ville, the old town, whatever space is not taken up by bistros and cafés goes to small craftsmen and visitor-oriented gift shops.

⬥ *Le Métropole is Monte Carlo's most upmarket shopping centre*

Eating & drinking

There's haute cuisine aplenty in central Monte Carlo, both in the dining rooms of the top hotels and in fashionable cafés and bistros. Many of these are attached to a major nightlife venue such as the Casino, the nearby Sporting d'Hiver, or the fashionable Sporting d'Eté summer club. But even in Monte Carlo, and certainly in nearly every other district of Monaco (with the possible exception of Moneghetti), there's no shortage of more affordable options for lunch and dinner. La Condamine offers perhaps the widest choice of cheap-to-medium-priced eating, both in the port area and just behind it, especially around Place d'Armes and its covered market. In residential Fontvieille most of the dining is on the waterfront, though there are one or two good options close to the park and the Roseraie Princesse Grace. Fontvieille has a large shopping complex (the Centre Commercial de Fontvieille) that offers a range of bars, cafés, low-cost brasseries and fast-food outlets. Monaco-Ville's narrow streets are full of cafés and bistros where the emphasis is often on traditional local cuisine.

Almost every kind of cooking style is available in cosmopolitan Monaco. The most popular flavours, understandably, are Provençal,

PRICE CATEGORIES
The following price guide, used throughout the book, indicates the average price per head for a two- to three-course dinner, excluding drinks. Lunch will usually be a little cheaper in each category.
£ up to €40 ££ €40–70 £££ over €70

🔵 *The grandest of grand restaurants – the Salle Empire at the Hôtel de Paris*

Italian and general Mediterranean, brought to a refined level in the top-class kitchens; but you don't have to go far to find Chinese, Japanese, Thai, Tex-Mex, North African and other regional cuisines, and even a few English-style pubs and Irish bars.

USEFUL DINING PHRASES

I would like a table for ... people
Je voudrais une table pour ... personnes
Zher voodray ewn tabl poor ... pehrson

Waiter/waitress!
Monsieur/Mademoiselle!
M'sewr/madmwahzel!

May I have the bill, please?
L'addition, s'il vous plaît
Ladissyohn, silvooplay

Could I have it well-cooked/medium/rare please?
Je le voudrais bien cuit/à point/saignant
Zher ler voodray beeang kwee/ah pwan/saynyong

I am a vegetarian. Does this contain meat?
Je suis végétarien (végétarienne). Est-ce que ce plat contient de la viande?
Zher swee vehzhehtariang (vehzhehtarien). Essker ser plah kontyang der lah vee-ond?

Where is the toilet (restroom), please?
Où sont les toilettes, s'il vous plaît?
Oo song lay twahlet, silvooplay?

Underneath this cosmopolitan fare, you can still find some truly Monégasque specialities in bakeries and takeaways all around town. These include *barbajuan*, a small pie filled with rice and squash, *fougasse*, a nut-topped pastry flavoured with orange-flower water, and *socca*, a chick-pea pancake that is a favourite street food in the markets. More substantial is *stocafi*, the local take on that favourite Mediterranean combination of salt cod, oil, tomatoes and black olives – at its most authentic in the little bistros of Monaco-Ville.

Even if these local dishes don't whet your appetite, the high quality of bread, fresh produce and *charcuterie* (prepared meats) in Monaco's markets and small shops, and even in the supermarkets of the shopping centres, should tempt you to take a picnic lunch to the beach or one of Monaco's green spaces.

Restaurant bills are often *service compris* (check for the phrase *sce compris* on your bill) – so unless you have had really good service, or you are dining in one of the very best restaurants, there's no need to tip. At most, you might leave the small change behind after a drink in a café. The major credit cards are accepted everywhere for all but the cheapest meals. By law, all restaurants and public places are non-smoking.

Strictly vegetarian establishments are thin on the ground, but Mediterranean and especially Italian cuisine, which is popular at all price levels, on the whole provides plenty of tasty non-meat and non-fish options, and most restaurants of any pretension will have specific vegetarian dishes on the menu.

Entertainment & nightlife

There is so much happening in Monaco, especially in Monte Carlo and especially in the summer months, that the following just scratches the surface. To get a full overview of what's on during your visit, make sure you call in at the tourist office for your copy of its invaluable monthly update *Bienvenue* as soon as you arrive. To make plans in advance visit Ⓦ www.visitmonaco.com

Think of Monte Carlo and you'll think of casinos. Even if you don't intend to gamble away the family silver on your trip, there's nothing to stop you paying the relatively modest fee to enter one of the Principality's high-class gaming halls and take in the atmosphere.

Of course the real high-roller games take place out of the public gaze, but there's still something irresistible about all the raw tension in the upmarket setting of the public tables. (If you're a member of the clergy, you needn't worry about compromising your principles – under Monégasque law they won't let you in anyway.) The lower age limit to enter a casino in Monaco is 21, and you'll need to bring your passport.

Monte Carlo has four grand and fashionable casinos, all owned by the Société des Bains de Mer (SBM), the company that Prince Charles III set up to run his new venture in the 1860s. (The SBM owns nearly every major public venue in Monte Carlo, in fact, including many of its best hotels – and the ruling family of Monaco owns two-thirds of the SBM.) In addition to the Casino de Monte-Carlo (see page 76), almost next door you'll find the Café de Paris and the Sun Casino (see pages 75 & 76); further north, past the Plage du Larvotto, is the Sporting d'Eté club, where the jet-setters frequent the Salle des Palmiers (see page 76) during July and August.

KNOW YOUR ROULETTE

For the uninitiated, French roulette is the kind where everybody crowds round the table, while the English version has a limited number of table seats and the players all bet in chips of their own colour. American roulette gives the bank two chances of taking everyone's money, with a 'o' and a 'oo' on the wheel.

The cinema is also a popular entertainment option in Monaco. The good news for English-speaking visitors is that both of Monaco's top cinemas often show films in *version originale* (VO), ie with their original soundtracks. So if they are showing the latest Hollywood release, you can hear it in English with French subtitles on the screen.

Monaco's coolest cinema – in every sense – is the **Cinéma d'Eté** (🅰 Terrasses du Parking des Pêcheurs 🕒 25 June–10 Sept 🚍 Bus: 1, 2 to Monaco Ville), its open-air cinema. Films are shown every evening in summer on the biggest outdoor screen in Europe, which is perched on the roof of the big car park at the tip of Monaco-Ville. For an indoor option, try the central three-screen **Cinema le Sporting** (🅰 Pl du Casino 🚍 Bus: 1, 2, 6 to Casino).

For details of other cinemas or to see what's on, check 🌐 www.cinemasporting.com or look in the monthly *Bienvenue* guide (see page 153).

Monte Carlo is home to Monaco's glitziest bars and nightclubs, while Fontvieille has the more relaxed, family-oriented venues, and La Condamine the studenty hangouts. Monaco's reputation for high-class glamour is mostly thanks to Monte Carlo's nightlife

○ *Reserve your table for dinner and entertainment at the Salle des Etoiles*

and it comes as a pleasant surprise to find that there is a lot more variety in Monaco than its reputation might suggest. The endearingly worn La Rascasse (see page 99), for instance, is an enormously popular bar, club and restaurant on the port attracting rock musicians, backpackers and everyone in between. La Condamine's Stars'N'Bars (see page 98) is a lively sports bar and was a popular haunt of Prince Albert II before he became ruler.

As well as casinos, cinemas, glam bars and discos, the other thing Monaco excels at is shows. If you fancy dressing up a bit and enjoying a traditional dinner and cabaret evening, then reserve your table at the Salle des Etoiles in the Sporting d'Eté club (see page 77). Check in particular whether there are any Gala Evenings planned: these are held frequently in aid of good causes and are the ultimate in glamour. There is nothing to stop you from dressing up to the nines and going along to enjoy top performers and rock bands while doing some serious celeb-spotting.

At the other end of the scale, there's a lively programme of outdoor entertainment called Le Fort Antoine dans la Ville, which sees concerts, spectacles and comedy performances all summer in Place d'Armes and elsewhere. For information on the current programme, see Ⓦ www.visitmonaco.com

Sport & relaxation

SPECTATOR SPORTS

A full programme of top-class sporting events kicks off with the Monte Carlo Rally in January (see page 9). April sees a tennis Masters tournament at the Monte-Carlo Country Club and the international show-jumping championship and, of course, May brings the Monaco Grand Prix (see page 12). Swimming takes over the arena in June, followed by Monaco Classic Week in September, an international event for classic yachts and motor boats. November rounds off the year with the Monaco International Marathon. If football is your sport, then go along to Stade Louis II to watch one of Europe's top clubs, AS Monaco.

PARTICIPATION SPORTS
Beaches & watersports

Monaco doesn't have the wide beaches of other resorts. The only one worthy of the name lies in the Principality itself – the public Plage du Larvotto (see page 67) at the far north of Monaco's coast. Further along Avenue Princesse Grace is Monte Carlo Beach, which is actually in France. In fact, most of the best beaches lie just outside Monaco, north and south along the Riviera.

On the other hand, Monaco provides top-class swimming facilities: two Olympic pools (Stade Nautique Rainier III and Stade Louis II – see pages 94 & 103), not to mention some excellent hotel pools, the Thermes Marins (see page 68) and even the municipal pool (⊕ 7 av St-Charles). Be advised that while topless sunbathing is tolerated, nude isn't. And make sure you change back to day clothes when you leave the beach – wearing swimwear on the streets is a definite no-no.

Bicycle & motorbike hire

You can hire a bicycle, scooter or motorbike for the day from **Holiday Bikes** (ⓐ Palais de la Scala, Galerie Commerciale, 1 av Henri Durand ⓣ 00 33 4 92 10 99 98 ⓦ www.rent-bike.fr).

Diving

Explore the underwater world of the Principality with the **Club d'Exploration Sousmarine** (ⓐ Cale de Halage, Port de Fontvieille ⓣ 99 99 99 60 ⓦ www.cesmm.com).

Golf

The nearest golf club is a 20-minute drive away in the hills behind Monaco. The **Monte-Carlo Golf Club** (ⓐ Mont Agel, La Turbie ⓣ 00 33 4 92 41 50 70) has an 18-hole course, par 71, and a practice range. You need a handicap of 35 (32 at weekends) to play there.

Tennis & squash

Two of the most popular clubs are the **Monte-Carlo Country Club** (ⓐ Av Princesse Grace, Roquebrune-Cap-Martin ⓣ 93 30 01 02 or 00 33 4 93 41 30 15 ⓦ www.mccc.mc), just across the border north of Larvotto, and **Monte-Carlo Squash Racket Club** in Fontvieille (ⓐ Stade Louis II, Av des Castelans ⓣ 92 05 42 22).

RELAXATION
Spas & fitness

Monaco has a number of upmarket spas, the best of which is the world-renowned Thermes Marins (see page 68). The spas attached to hotels tend to have their own menu. The Thermes Marins' restaurant 'L'Hirondelle' is the best for healthy options.

Accommodation

Monaco offers over 2,100 hotel beds in categories ranging from the highest luxury, clustered around the Casino, down to three- and two-star establishments in the outlying areas of the Principality, especially La Condamine; the latter include motels and representatives of chains such as Ibis. There are no youth hostels, backpacker hotels or campsites within the borders of the Principality, though; if you're on a really tight budget your best option is to stay at a hostel or campsite in one of the neighbouring French Riviera resorts, for example around Nice, and travel into Monaco, making use of its excellent transport links. This applies equally to hotels: you may find a hotel closer to your requirements and at a better rate just outside the Principality, at Menton or along the Nice–Monaco stretch of the Riviera, for instance.

Breakfast is almost always charged extra; upmarket hotels lay on a full buffet, but some others stick to the continental minimum of coffee, juice and bread. If your hotel doesn't provide the kind of breakfast you want, take your *petit déjeuner* at a café instead (many of which also offer an 'English' or 'American' breakfast).

Unless you have booked an inclusive package, it pays to investigate thoroughly on the web; in addition to hotels' own web pages and

PRICE CATEGORIES

The following ratings indicate the average price for a double room per night – some rooms may be more or less expensive than the rating suggests.

£ up to €150   **££** €150–300   **£££** over €300 (note: rates in the grandest hotels can be considerably over this level)

the many hotel-finder sites, the tourist office offers listings and instant reservations at Ⓦ www.visitmonaco.com. Special packages and offers, especially for the quieter seasons, abound. Listed below are a few recommendations, but there are plenty of other good hotels to choose from.

HOTELS

Hôtel de France £ Situated in the La Condamine area, this hotel offers 26 rooms with all the basic facilities and pleasant, if unremarkable, décor. Ⓐ 6 rue de la Turbie (La Condamine & Moneghetti) Ⓣ 93 30 24 64 Ⓦ www.monte-carlo.mc/france Ⓝ Bus: 1, 2, 4, 5, 6 to Place d'Armes

Le Versailles £ A two-star hotel situated, like most others in its category, in La Condamine, Le Versailles has just 15 rooms and a large restaurant. Ⓐ 4 av Prince-Pierre (La Condamine & Moneghetti) Ⓣ 93 50 79 34 Ⓦ www.monte-carlo.mc/versailles Ⓝ Bus: 1, 2, 4, 5, 6 to Place d'Armes

Novotel £–££ Conveniently located next to the train station, this simple yet stylish hotel has great facilities including a fitness centre, Turkish bath, swimming pool and restaurant. Great value. Ⓐ 16 blvd de la Princesse Charlotte (La Condamine & Moneghetti) Ⓣ 99 99 83 00 Ⓦ www.novotel.com

Ambassador-Monaco ££ Housed in a 19th-century building, the Ambassador has 35 rooms and an Italian restaurant, as well as a private beach for summer guests. Ⓐ 10 av Prince-Pierre (La Condamine & Moneghetti) Ⓣ 97 97 96 96 Ⓦ www.ambassadormonaco.com Ⓝ Bus: 1, 2, 4, 5, 6 to Place d'Armes

● *Relax in one of the pools at Le Méridien Beach Plaza*

Miramar ££ Nicely situated close to the harbour, the Miramar has just 11 rooms, all with sea views, a restaurant and a wine/tapas bar. ⓐ 1 av du Président Kennedy (Monte Carlo) ❶ 93 30 86 48 ⓦ www.miramarmonaco.com ❷ Bus: 1, 2, 6 to Ostende

Ni Hôtel ££ This boutique hotel next to the Rock of Monaco offers 17 ultra-modern rooms. Its fashionable Ni Bar is perfect for an aperitif. ⓐ 1 bis rue Grimaldi (La Condamine & Moneghetti) ❶ 97 97 51 51 ⓦ www.nihotel.com ❷ Bus: 1, 2, 4, 5, 6 to Place d'Armes

Columbus Monaco ££–£££ Although it markets itself particularly as a business/conference venue, this chic 181-room hotel has a lot to offer leisure tourists who want something stylish at an affordable price. Situated in Fontvieille, it has views of the sea and the Roseraie Princesse Grace, and offers a fitness area and outdoor pool. ⓐ 23 av des Papalins (Fontvieille) ⓣ 92 05 90 00 ⓦ www.columbusmonaco.com ⓝ Bus: 5 to Papalins

Le Méridien Beach Plaza ££–£££ If relaxation is high on your agenda then this hotel-resort's three swimming pools and private beach may be just what you're looking for. All of the 403 rooms have their own private balcony and most have sea views, and in addition to the year-round rooftop restaurant there's an informal buffet-grill in the summer. ⓐ 22 av Princesse-Grace (Monte Carlo) ⓣ 93 30 98 80 ⓦ www.lemeridienmontecarlo.com ⓝ Bus: 6 to Larvotto

Hôtel Métropole £££ A recent refurbishment has transformed the Métropole into one of Monaco's most romantic hotels. Refitted to resemble the interior of a Venetian palazzo, the new Métropole is sumptuous and houses the Michelin-starred Joël Robuchon restaurant. ⓐ 4 av de la Madone (Monte Carlo) ⓣ 93 15 15 15 ⓦ www.metropole.com ⓝ Bus: 1, 2, 6 to Casino

Hôtel de Paris £££ One of the original de-luxe hotels built for the first guests of the Casino, this legendary establishment has a guestbook filled with famous names from the last century and a half. Service and accommodation is totally up to date, however. One of its three restaurants is chef Alain Ducasse's Louis XV (see page 72) in La Salle Empire, an architectural as well as a gastronomic tour de force. ⓐ Pl du Casino (Monte Carlo) ⓣ 98 06 30 00 ⓦ www.hotel deparismontecarlo.com ⓝ Bus: 1, 2, 6 to Casino

Monte-Carlo Bay Hotel & Resort £££ The SBM's newest project, the Monte-Carlo Bay Hotel is Monaco's grandest resort hotel. Built to rival the ambitious resorts springing up in Dubai, it is located next to Jimmy'z nightclub and the Sporting d'Eté – and has several new restaurants (of which the Blue Bay is the crowning glory), as well as an incredible multi-level swimming pool. 🅰 40 Av Princesse Grace (Monte Carlo) 🅣 98 06 02 00 🅦 www.montecarlobay.com 🅝 Bus: 6 to Larvotto

Monte Carlo Beach Hotel £££ With just 47 rooms, this is one of the smaller luxury hotels in Monaco, a 1930s resort tucked away by the sea on the northern tip of the bay of Monaco, just outside the Principality's borders. It boasts three restaurants and a private beach. 🅰 Av Princesse Grace, Roquebrune-Cap-Martin 🅣 93 28 66 66 🅦 www.monte-carlo-beach.com 🅛 Mar–mid-Nov

SELF-CATERING

For stays of a week or more, and especially if you're travelling as a family, it may well be worth considering renting a villa or an apartment. Again, there is plenty of help available on the web, but a particularly useful resource for apartments just outside Monaco, at Cap d'Ail and Beausoleil, is 🅦 www.monaco-hotel.com (navigate to 'Résidences')

If you are looking for a very central location and expense is not a concern, then the following luxury apartment is available for rent by the week or longer (or for purchase on a time-share basis):
Le Castel Residence £££ Located on the hillside overlooking La Condamine and the sea, with magnificent views of the Rocher de Monaco (Rock of Monaco). 🅰 9 av Corvetto Frères (Monte Carlo) 🅣 97 97 12 97 🅦 www.lecastel.com

⬤ *The doyen of Monte Carlo hotels occupies the best position in town*

THE BEST OF MONTE CARLO & MONACO

TOP 10 SIGHTS & EXPERIENCES

- **Casino de Monte-Carlo** You don't have to be a gambler to visit the world-famous institution that is virtually synonymous with Monte Carlo (see page 64).

- **Palais Princier (Prince's Palace)** Tour the state apartments of the Grimaldis and absorb the history of this tiny but independent country (see page 81).

- **Dinner for two** It could be the acme of haute cuisine at one of Monte Carlo's grandest hotels or a simple meal at a small restaurant overlooking one of Monaco's two harbours.

- **Roseraie Princesse Grace** Recharge your spiritual batteries in this fragrant haven, tucked away in quiet Fontvieille (see page 103).

- **Spa treatment** Treat yourself to renewal and a sense of well-being from the therapies of the Thermes Marins (see page 68) or any one of Monte Carlo's other luxurious spas.

- **Salle des Etoiles** Put on your glad rags and rub shoulders with the rich and famous at one of this legendary venue's Gala Evenings (see page 77).

- **Musée Océanographique** A world-class museum of marine life with fascinating aquarium and shark tank (see page 84).

- **Jardin Exotique & Grotte de L'Observatoire** Two contrasting experiences in one place – an internationally acclaimed garden of amazing plants and a deep, stalagmite-filled cave once inhabited by Stone Age man (see page 90)

- **Dance the night away** Waltz and whirl in glamorous company at clubs such as Jimmy'z (see page 73) or at the Grimaldi Forum (see page 65).

- **Watch the Grand Prix** Reserve a trackside table at a restaurant overlooking the course and enjoy the drama of the race over a leisurely lunch (see page 12).

🔻 *Boats and yachts in Monaco's harbour*

Suggested itineraries

HALF-DAY: MONACO IN A HURRY

If you're just calling into Monaco on a longer Riviera holiday, or maybe indulging in a spot of sightseeing during a business trip, then make for Place du Casino in the very heart of Monte Carlo. Visit the Casino itself and take time to stroll around the gardens that front it before exploring the multicoloured Terrasse du Casino, taking in its views over the harbour of Port Hercule. Lunch before or after should ideally be at the old-world Café de Paris.

1 DAY: TIME TO SEE A LITTLE MORE

If you have more than half a day, then add to your sightseeing itinerary the old town of Monaco-Ville. It's easy to reach the far end of the Rocher de Monaco (Rock of Monaco), as buses 1 and 2 terminate there. Wander through the narrow streets, which seem to inhabit a different time and place from the glitz and bustle of Monte Carlo. Don't forget to emerge at the Jardins St-Martin on the south side of the Rock for great views over the coast and harbour of Fontvieille, before continuing to the cathedral where Princess Grace is buried. End your stroll at the Place du Palais and take time out to tour the Palais Princier.

2–3 DAYS: TIME TO SEE MUCH MORE

With more time in hand you can visit some of the attractions in Monaco-Ville (start with the Musée Océanographique) and the nearby Terrasses de Fontvieille, with its collections of vintage cars, scale-model ships and Monégasque stamps and coins. You should also make time to see the Jardin Exotique and Grotte de l'Observatoire with its attendant museum of early mankind.

Alternatively, take the bus into Fontvieille and drink in the tranquillity of the Roseraie Princesse Grace and the Parc Paysager, with its intriguing assembly of sculptures. While you're there you may want to take a helicopter tour from the nearby heliport. This still leaves time during your stay for shopping in La Condamine (and, if your credit card allows, Monte Carlo's designer emporia), and you can fit in some self-indulgent physical refreshment at one of Monaco's spas or beauty and fitness centres. In the evenings, party in the nightclubs and bars of Monte Carlo, and on the harbour front, or take in a show or a game of roulette at the Casino.

LONGER: ENJOYING MONACO TO THE FULL

You'll want to return to some of the places on the 2–3-day schedule, to see them by both day and night, but a longer visit allows you to explore the lesser delights of the Principality as well. You can also take off from Monaco Ville rail station for destinations along the Riviera, such as Menton and Ventimiglia.

● *There are many great places to explore on the Riviera, such as Menton*

Something for nothing

Despite its pricey reputation, you don't have to bankrupt yourself to enjoy Monaco and, although there is an entrance fee to most of its attractions (usually a fairly modest one), many of the best experiences come at little or no charge.

For such a built-up area, Monaco offers some excellent walking, both in its beautifully maintained parks and open spaces (all free) and out along the coastal paths of the Riviera, either southwards, from Fontvieille to Cap d'Ail, or north from Monte Carlo Beach to Cap-Martin (each taking about three hours there and back along the villa-studded shoreline). Football fans will have an extra treat if they take the Champions Promenade, a 40-minute walk along

CHEMIN DES SCULPTURES (SCULPTURE TRAIL)

As you stroll through Monaco, you can't fail to notice the modern sculptures that adorn the streets. Some of them are grotesque, some hilarious, some poignant, and many are truly beautiful works of art. Together they represent a massive, free-of-charge outdoor exhibition of the work of the world's best-known modern sculptors. The full trail, comprising more than 100 works, extends the whole length of the Principality, from the Plage du Larvotto to Fontvieille, though the greatest concentration is to be found around the Parc Paysager and Roseraie Princesse Grace in Fontvieille (see page 103). You can even get an illustrated guide to them all from the tourist office. Following the trail makes a great themed walking tour of Monaco that won't cost you a penny.

Monaco's own shore, from Monte Carlo Beach to Port Hercule: the footprints of the world's most famous footballers have been moulded into the ground along the way. See if you can spot Roberto Baggio, Pelé, Alfredo Di Stéfano, Michel Platini and George Best.

The medieval streets of the old town are a walker's and photographer's delight, and they all end eventually at the Rocher de Monaco, the promontory on which Monaco-Ville is built, looking out to great views of the two harbours and the Riviera coast.

◯ *You'll meet Botero's* Adam and Eve *on the Chemin des Sculptures*

When it rains

There won't be many days when rain stops play in Monaco, as the Principality enjoys some of the best weather in Europe. Showers are usually over quickly, giving you a good excuse to stop for coffee but not ruining your day.

If you are unlucky enough to be caught in a prolonged downpour, however, there are plenty of indoor attractions. The resort's museums are varied and have something for every interest and age group. You could easily spend a full morning or afternoon in the Musée Océanographique (see page 84), with its shark tank and other aquaria; the Palais Princier and its attendant museums (see page 81) likewise make a good half-day visit, and if your interests run that way, it's easy to lose track of time in the Musée Naval or the Collection des Voitures Anciennes (see page 105).

Alternatively, get under cover in the Métropole shopping centre in Monte Carlo (see page 69) and shop till you drop – you can always window-shop if the price tags are too high, and it has plenty of cafés and bars where you can people-watch.

If the weather is wet, why not get wet anyway? Monaco is blessed with high-quality swimming pools, such as the Stade Nautique Rainier III (see page 94) and the Stade Louis II in Fontvieille (page 103). Or make this the day to treat yourself to some self-indulgent pampering in one of the area's many excellent spas, such as the Thermes Marins (see page 68), or build up a sweat in their well-equipped gyms.

If that all sounds too much like hard work, simply find a cosy table at the Café de Paris or another high temple of cuisine and sample some of the best cooking on the Continent. And don't forget, the casinos are always open.

🔺 *When it rains it's good to get underwater at the Musée Océanographique*

On arrival

TIME DIFFERENCE
Monaco follows Central European Time (CET). During Daylight Saving Time (end Mar–end Oct), the clocks are put ahead by one hour.

ARRIVING
By air
The air gateway to Monaco is 25 km (15 miles) away at Nice Côte d'Azur Airport. The airport is the second largest in France in terms of passengers (eight million a year) but it's a manageable size and gets its customers landside pretty quickly. In each of the two terminals there are two banks to take care of any foreign exchange needs, open 08.45–23.00 daily.

The coolest, fastest and most expensive way to get from the airport to Monaco is by helicopter. Seventy flights per day go direct from the airport to Monaco's **heliport** (ⓐ Av des Ligures ⓣ 92 05 00 50 ⓦ www.heliairmonaco.com ⓛ Flights depart every 30 mins), taking just seven minutes and costing around €125 for a single trip or around €220 for a return. Reserving in advance is a good idea. From the heliport, a shuttle bus will take you to your hotel.

A more mundane way to get from the airport to Monaco is by taxi, which takes around 35 minutes and costs between €75 and €100. A cheaper but still convenient option is the express bus (Nice–Menton line 110), which takes around 50 minutes and costs €18 one way. The non-express bus (Nice–Menton line 100) costs just €1 one way. There is a night bus, the NocTAM'bus (ⓦ www.rca.tm.fr), which departs from Terminal 1 Thur–Sat 22.00–02.30. Tell the driver where you want to get off. The other option is the train, which departs from St Augustin station, a ten-minute walk from the airport

△ *Arrive in style at the heliport*

terminal. Take the local TER train direct to Monaco's central railway station (see page 59); the journey takes around 30 minutes and a single adult fare is currently €4.80.

Car-hire firms at the airport include Avis, Budget, Europcar, Hertz, National/Citer and Sixt; the pick-up point is outside Terminal 2 (reached from Terminal 1 via the free shuttle bus).

Nice Côte d'Azur Airport ⊕ 0820 423 333 for flight information ⓦ www.nice.aeroport.fr

By rail

The international SNCF rail station is located at Avenue Prince-Pierre in the Condamine district, which is where the majority of two- and three-star hotels are clustered. It's a short taxi ride from there to the other districts. See page 59 for more information on the station and rail connections.

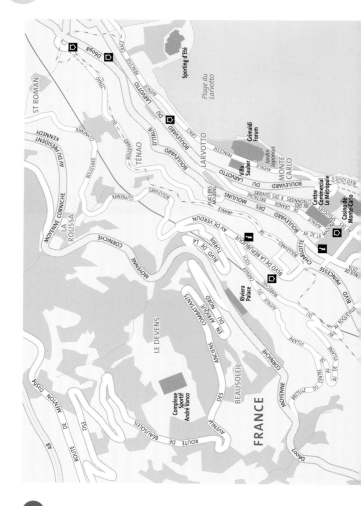

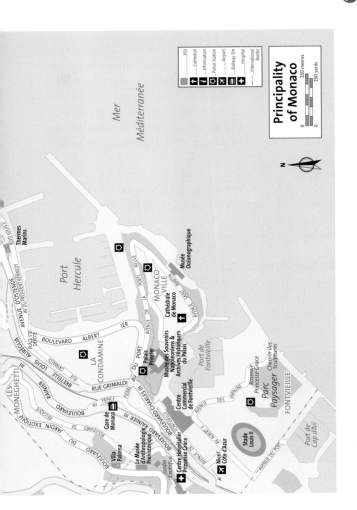

By road

The France–Italy A8 motorway skirts Monaco. If approaching from the west turn off at junction 56, signposted Monaco, or from the east at the Monaco-Roquebrune-Cap-Martin exit. If you don't mind sharp bends, leave the motorway earlier and get on to the Moyenne Corniche coastal road for great views. There are plenty of car parks within Monaco; many of the smaller hotels don't have their own parking but are seldom far away from a large public car park.

By sea

Cruise ships dock at Port Hercule, right in the middle of Monaco, flanked by the rock of Monaco-Ville on one side and Monte Carlo on the other. There are plenty of buses from the harbour to Monte Carlo and Monaco-Ville (alternatively, just hop on a lift to reach the latter).

FINDING YOUR FEET

Monaco puts itself out to be helpful to visitors, and in a country so small it's hard to get lost. The presence of so much money ensures that streets are safe and clean, with few undesirable characters, and there are plenty of policemen on hand. Make sure you don't

● The Moyenne Corniche is the scenic approach to Monaco

unwittingly cause problems. You don't have to dress glamorously but you should try to look respectable: bare chests, bare feet and swimwear are illegal in public anywhere but the beach. And don't upset the *gendarmes* (policemen) by crossing against traffic signals or away from authorised pedestrian crossings.

ORIENTATION

Monaco is basically a small strip of coastline bordered on all sides by France. Its two harbours, the main Port Hercule (also called Port de Monaco) and the smaller yacht harbour of Port de Fontvieille, divide the coastline into three distinct areas. Jutting out between the two

---

IF YOU GET LOST, TRY ...

Excuse me, do you speak English?
Excusez-moi, parlez-vous anglais?
Ekskewzeh-mwah, pahrlay-voo onglay?

Excuse me, is this the right way to the old town/the city centre/the tourist office/the station/the bus station?
Excusez-moi, c'est la bonne direction pour la vieille ville/
le centre-ville/l'office de tourisme/la gare/gare routière?
Ekskewzeh-mwah, seh lah bon deereksee-ong poor lah vee-ay veel/ler songtr veel/lohfeece de tooreezm/lah gahr/gahr rootyair?

Can you point to it on my map?
Pouvez-vous me le montrer sur la carte?
Poovayvoo mer ler mawngtreh sewr lah kart?

---

ports is the rocky plateau of the old town; the correct name for this quarter is simply Monaco, but to avoid confusion with the Principality as a whole it is often referred to by its alternative name of Monaco-Ville (it is also known as the Rocher de Monaco, the Rock of Monaco). Dominated by the Palais Princier (Prince's Palace, see page 81) and distinguished by its elegant 18th-century houses painted in pastel shades, Monaco-Ville is the original area of the Principality and is still where the oldest native Monégasque families live. Facing Monaco-Ville, across the smaller harbour to which it gives its name, is the newest district, largely built on reclaimed land, the suburb of Fontvieille. This is mainly a residential area of high-rise, high-priced apartments, but it possesses some visitor attractions too, such as the Roseraie Princesse Grace (see page 103). North of Port Hercule is Monte Carlo, created in 1866 by, and named after, Prince Charles III, which is the glamorous end of the Principality, home to the Casino and other high-society hotels, bars and restaurants.

At the centre of inland Monaco, extending back from Port Hercule, lies La Condamine. The second-oldest area of Monaco (the name refers to the cultivated land that originally supplied the needs of the castle), this is a district of hotels and shops, which also contains the railway station. Behind La Condamine, the suburb of Moneghetti climbs up into the hillside. North along the coast beyond Monte Carlo lies Larvotto, extending from its separate bay, with Monaco's largest beach, back to the national border with the French municipality of Roquebrune-Cap-Martin.

GETTING AROUND

The entire coastline of Monaco is just over 4 km (2 ½ miles) in length, and the city extends inland an average of 1 km (just over ½ mile). It is therefore quite feasible to visit most of what the city has to offer on

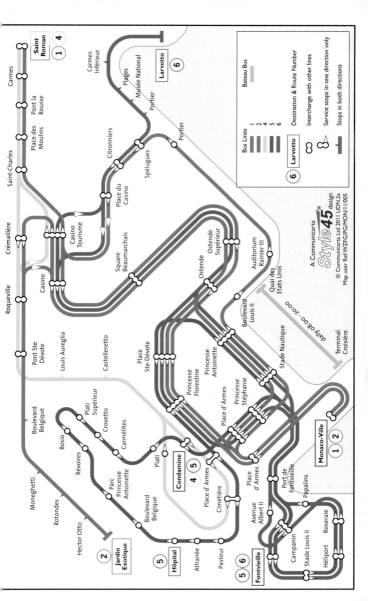

TOP TOURS

To get a speedy overview of what Monaco has to offer, one option is a ready-made tour. In addition to the helicopter trips described on page 100, there are two tour options – one cheap, one rather expensive.

Tourist train A quick way of discovering the secrets of the old town is to take the little red-and-white tourist 'train' that departs from outside the Musée Océanographique for a 30-minute tour of Monaco-Ville. ☎ 92 05 64 38 🕐 10.00–17.00 daily (summer); 10.30–17.00 daily (winter)

Monte-Carlo Limousine If you have the urge to do things in style, splash out on your own personal guided tour in a limousine with a multilingual chauffeur/guide. 🏠 Fairmont Monte Carlo Hotel, 12 av des Spélugues ☎ 93 50 82 65

foot. The steepness of its coastal geography would be a drawback for pedestrian sightseeing if it weren't for the public lifts that link various parts of the city, including the Centre Hospitalier Princesse Grace and the Jardin Exotique; Port Hercule and Avenue de la Costa; Place Ste-Devote and Moneghetti; Avenue des Citronniers and Avenue Grande-Bretagne; Boulevard Rainier III and Boulevard du Larvotto. There is a lift in Place des Moulins and another linking the Terrasse du Casino with the Congress Centre Auditorium and Boulevard Louis II.

For less energetic or longer travel around Monaco, there is a small but excellent bus system of just five lines (numbered 1, 2, 4, 5 and 6 – there's no Line 3) that carries over 5 million passengers a year. Lines 1 and 2 connect Monaco-Ville with Monte Carlo's Casino (Line 1 continues to St-Roman on the northern border). Lines 4 and 5 both connect the railway station with the city – Line 4 goes to Monte Carlo while Line 5 heads in the other direction to Fontvieille. Line 6 traverses the entire coastline from Fontvieille, via the main harbour and the Casino and on to Larvotto. Buses run every 11 minutes or so between around 07.00 and 21.00 from Monday to Saturday, and every 20 minutes between 07.30 and 21.00 on Sundays and public holidays. You can buy single tickets from the driver but it's better value to purchase either a day travel card (€3) or a ten-journey card (€6). For more information call ☎ 97 70 22 22 or see 🌐 www.cam.mc

TER (regional French railway) trains from the **central railway station** (🚆 Av Prince-Pierre, La Condamine) provide an easy, and remarkably cheap, way to visit the Riviera beyond Monaco. There are at least 20 trains a day in both directions, allowing quick access east to Menton (approx 12 mins) and the Italian town of Ventimiglia (24 mins) and west to Nice (25 mins) and many other resorts, as far as Cannes (1 hr 10 mins). Not all trains stop at every station on the line, so pick up a free timetable. Tickets can be purchased at easy-to-use machines at all stops. **Train reservation and information** ☎ 08 00 83 59 23 🌐 www.ter-sncf.com/paca

Driving within the centre of Monaco could be slower than walking, but if you are staying outside the centre and driving in every day, you won't find any shortage of car parks, many of them with CCTV surveillance. On-street parking is restricted and the *gendarmes* are very fussy about not only where you park but also how tidily you park! Monaco roads operate on a one-way system, so finding your way can be a little tricky even for seasoned drivers. Note that access by car to Monaco-Ville is restricted to cars registered in Monaco or the Alpes-Maritimes *département* of France.

Taxis are available 24 hours daily by calling ☎ 08 20 20 98 98. There are also taxi ranks at the exits to the rail station, the Casino, Avenue des Papalins in Fontvieille, near the Hotel Méridien Beach

Plaza in Larvotto, Avenue. du President Kennedy at Port Hercule, and several other strategic points around Monaco.

Car hire

If you want to hire a car, it's usually better and cheaper to do it in advance through your travel agent or airline or one of the main rental companies' central booking systems on the web. If it's a spur-of-the-moment decision, Avis, Hertz and Europcar, and five local companies, have offices in Monaco itself – the tourist office can provide a full list. For airport car rentals, see page 51.

You may want to hire a chauffeur-driven limo to turn up at the Casino or the Café de Paris – more impressive than getting off the bus. There are 11 companies who provide this service.

Or perhaps you want to live a fantasy millionaire lifestyle for a day or two (and this is certainly the place to do it); you can hire a swanky self-drive limousine or sports car from **Elite Rent a Car** (❸ 34 quai Jean-Charles-Rey ❶ 97 77 33 11 Ⓦ www.eliterent.com).

Guided tours

Some companies offer sightseeing tours of Monaco and the French and Italian Rivieras in a minibus, with an English-speaking driver. One of them is **Dream Tours** (❸ 57 rue Grimaldi ❶ 97 77 78 79 Ⓦ www.dream-tours.com).

The **Grand Tour of Monaco** is a tour around Monaco's principal tourist sites on board an open-top bus with a running commentary in English. There are 12 stops and you can hop on or off the bus at will (🕘 10.00–18.00 daily; every 15 mins in summer, every 30 mins in winter ❶ 97 70 26 36).

▶ *Monaco perches precariously between mountain and sea*

THE CITY & PRINCIPALITY OF
Monaco

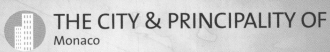

Monte Carlo

This is the district that has made Monaco famous; the very name conjures up images of fortunes being won and lost at the gambling tables in surroundings of unparalleled luxury. The original name, Plateau des Spélugues, would never have had the same ring to it. It was Charles III who, having decided to repair the state's fortunes with one of history's earliest large-scale leisure developments, named the area after himself – 'Charles' Hill' in Italian. It could be argued that the other Charles who is commemorated in the name is the French architect Charles Garnier. Monte Carlo is dominated by the buildings Garnier designed, including not only the Casino and Opéra but also the impressive Musée National.

CHARLES GARNIER

Charles Garnier (1825–1898) was born of humble origins in Paris. After working his way up as a draughtsman he entered the Ecole des Beaux-Arts, and studied for five years at the Academy in Rome, gaining inspiration from the grandeur of ancient Roman architecture. While still a humble municipal architect, Garnier entered and won the competition to design the new Paris Opéra in 1861. His vision, marked by drama, colour and decorative detail, reflected the grandiose aspirations of Napoleon III's Second Empire and his career never looked back. Garnier quickly became the architect of choice for large prestige projects of the period and was eagerly sought by his namesake, Charles III of Monaco, to create the impressive array of public buildings that still characterise Monte Carlo today.

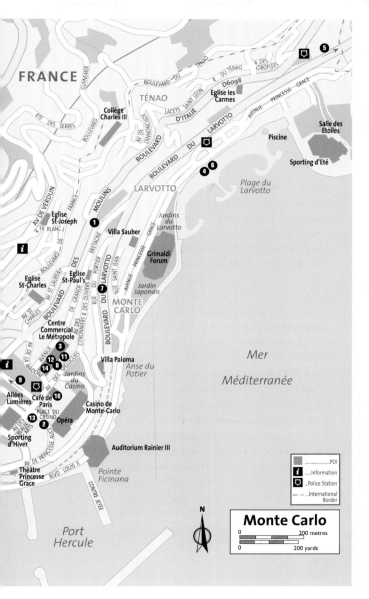

The northernmost suburb of Monaco, Larvotto, is in many ways an extension of Monte Carlo and is included in this chapter. It has few attractions of its own but is blessed with a large beach, and its nightlife in summer is centred on the large Sporting d'Eté.

SIGHTS & ATTRACTIONS

Casino de Monte-Carlo

Built by Garnier in 1878, the world's most famous temple to the Goddess of Fortune would be an attraction even without the glamour of what goes on inside. The impressive façade is set off by a large garden of flowerbeds and ponds surrounded by manicured lawns, extending from the front of the Casino gently upwards towards the town. At the rear is an even larger multicoloured terrace of geometric patterns designed by the artist Vasarely, which forms the roof of the convention centre and auditorium below, and is part of Monaco's Chemin des Sculptures (see pages 46 and 103).

Opulent is the only way to describe the Casino's interior, with its wealth of gold leaf, ornate plasterwork, frescoes and sculptures. The marble-paved atrium is surrounded by 28 Ionic columns in onyx. It leads into the recently renovated Salle Garnier, the red-and-gold auditorium of the Opéra, which opened in 1879 with a performance by Sarah Bernhardt and has been the scene of international-standard opera, ballet and concerts ever since.

The gaming area of the Casino consists of a succession of rooms featuring stained-glass windows, admirable decorations and sculptures, allegorical paintings and bronze lamps.

If you're not into gambling and just want to visit the Casino rather than play there, it's still advisable to dress smartly (a jacket and tie is obligatory for men). It costs nothing to visit, though.

ⓐ Pl du Casino ☎ 98 06 21 21 Ⓦ www.montecarlocasinos.com
🕐 From 14.00 daily ⓝ Bus: 1, 2, 6 to Casino

Eglise St-Charles (St Charles' Church)

A few blocks away from the Casino, at the very edge of Monte Carlo and of the Principality, stands the church that Charles III built for his patron saint in 1883 in a style officially described as French Renaissance. (The dearth of authentic medieval churches is a reminder of how recent the origins of Monaco's wealth are.) Its highlights include the 36-m (108-ft) bell tower, 19 stained-glass windows and the gilded chandeliers which used to decorate the Palace Throne Room. There is a Sunday service in English at 12.00. ⓐ Av Saint-Charles ☎ 93 30 74 90 🕐 10.00–12.00, 16.00–18.00 Tues–Sat and for religious ceremonies ⓝ Bus: 1, 4 to Saint-Charles

Grimaldi Forum

The Grimaldi Forum's original purpose as a super-luxurious conference centre has been somewhat eclipsed by its popularity as a concert venue. The Grimaldi also plays host to a number of star-studded awards ceremonies, including the Monte-Carlo Television Festival. Its many superb exhibitions often spill out on to its seafront terrace. ⓐ 10 av Princesse Grace ☎ 99 99 21 00 Ⓦ www.grimaldiforum.com ⓝ Bus: 6 to Musée National

Jardin Japonais (Japanese Garden)

Follow the winding Avenue des Spélugues around the garden of the Casino and on to Avenue Princesse Grace to reach the Jardin Japonais, an oasis of serenity that is spiritually a million miles from the glitz of Place du Casino. Designed by the landscape architect Yasuo Beppu, the garden is a living work of art that covers 2,300 sq m

🔺 *The Jardin Japonais provides some welcome tranquillity in Monte Carlo*

(25,000 sq ft) and has been blessed by a Shinto High Priest. Stone, water and plants have been combined in the harmony for which the Japanese garden design is famous. In early spring look out for the flowering of the wealth of azaleas, rhododendrons and camellias.

🅐 Av Princesse Grace 🕐 09.00–sunset daily 🚌 Bus: 6 to Portier

Nouveau Musée National de Monaco

Opened in 2010, Monaco's new visual arts museum (Ⓦ www. nmnm.mc) displays items from its collection following a programme of exhibitions in two different buildings. **Villa Sauber**, located in the Larvotto area, is used to hold exhibitions on the theme of 'art and performance'. 🅐 17 av Princesse Grace 🕐 98 98 91 26 🕐 10.00–18.00 daily 🚌 Bus: 6 to Musée National; or 1 or 4 to Pl des Moulins and take the lift ⓘ Admission charge

    Villa Paloma, a beautiful white villa on the edge of the Parc Princesse Antoinette, is used for exhibitions to do with 'art and

territory'. ⓐ 15 blvd du Jardin Exotique ⓣ 98 98 48 60 ⓛ 10.00–
18.00 daily (Sept–June); 11.00–19.00 daily (July & Aug) ⓝ Bus: 2 or 5
to Hector Otto ⓘ Admission charge

Place du Casino (Casino Square)

The square is *the* place to see celebrities, real or wannabe, and the
seriously wealthy. This is the social hub of Monte Carlo, where high-
rollers alight from their chauffeur-driven sports cars and limousines.
The venerable Café de Paris flanks one side of the square, and the
Hôtel de Paris, one of the original luxury hotels built at the same
time as the Casino, faces it on the other side.

Plage du Larvotto

The Plage du Larvotto is strictly speaking the only beach in Monaco.
The many others lie on or just beyond the border. Much of this free
beach is now given over to semi-private areas, where you can rent
deckchairs and order food and cocktails to be brought to you. The best
of these areas is at La Note Bleue (see page 70). A quarter of an hour's
walk down the same street leads you to its snazzy sister, the Monte
Carlo Beach where you'll pay an admission fee. If you want to have a
look around first, say you're just going to its (excellent) Sea Lounge bar,
which has free entry and is worth a visit in its own right. ⓐ Beach
access from Av Princesse Grace ⓝ Bus: 6 to Plages

SPAS, BEAUTY SALONS & FITNESS CENTRES

Monte Carlo offers its visitors a wealth of facilities to help them
feel good and look good. Other establishments offer a wide range of
beauty treatments, keep-fit programmes and massages. Here are
just a few.

Beauty Spa Daniela Steiner Manicures, pedicures, anti-cellulite treatment and slimming programmes. ❷ 1 av de Grande Bretagne ❶ 97 77 13 66 ⓦ www.steinercosmetics.com ⓛ 09.00–19.00 daily

Centre de Fitness Trained staff using state-of-the-art equipment will put you through your own tailor-made fitness programme. ❷ Fairmont Monte Carlo Hotel, 12 av des Spélugues ❶ 93 50 65 00 ⓛ 06.30–22.00 daily

Espace Beauté Eric Zemmour You can glam up and get yourself some hair extensions before a night at the casino in this trendy hairdressing salon. It also does manicures and foot care. ❷ 6 blvd des Moulins ❶ 97 70 01 91 ⓦ http://ericzemmour.com ⓛ 09.00–19.00 Mon–Sat

Monte Carlo Gym Aerobics gym, body-building and stretching. ❷ 6 blvd des Moulins ❶ 93 25 85 58 ⓦ www.montecarlo gym.com ⓛ 09.00–21.00 daily

Sunshine Yoga Private and group classes in yoga of all kinds. ❷ 40 av Princesse Grace ❶ 97 77 78 01 ⓦ www.yogamontecarlo.com ⓛ See website for class times

Thermes Marins If you're looking for the ultimate in pampering, or want expert help easing aches and pains, then the Thermes Marins is for you. Facing on to the sea and just round the corner from the Hôtel de Paris and the Casino, it offers every kind of health, relaxation and beauty treatment: seawater therapies such as calming marine baths and hydromassage, hi-tech cardio training, an enormous swimming pool, a solarium, hammam and sauna. Le Salon Bleu is a combined beauty and hairdressing salon, L'Hirondelle restaurant serves up low-calorie gastronomy, and you can stock up on vitamins with one of the Atlantide bar's cocktails. To get all the benefits, you should sign up for a six- or seven-day programme, but there are also one-day sessions. ⓐ 2 av de Monte-Carlo ⓣ 98 06 69 00 ⓦ www.monte carlothalasso.com ⓛ 08.00–20.00 daily

RETAIL THERAPY

For most of us, Monte Carlo will be more for window shopping than actual purchases. The so-called '**Golden Square**' of Avenue de Monte-Carlo, Avenue Beaux-Arts and Allées Lumières is home to some of the most famous names in fashion and design: Hermès, Céline, Christian Dior, Yves Saint Laurent, Louis Vuitton, Gucci, Chanel, Prada, Ichthys, and the list goes on. **Place du Casino** and nearby streets major on jewellery: Cartier, Chopard, Van Cleef & Arpels, Bulgari and Piaget are just some of the names here. Antiques and fine arts, naturally, are much in evidence, as well as stores displaying the very latest in interior design and tableware. The **Métropole** shopping centre just off the square has 80 or so boutiques, as well as cafés and bars catering to weary shoppers. This is also where you will find a branch of FNAC, the well-known French chain that combines CDs, books, computers and other electronic products with a ticket agency, and a supermarket for food shopping. Away from the Casino area, towards the Eglise St-Charles (see page 65) is where you will find the bakers, *charcutiers* and greengrocers of Monte Carlo.

TAKING A BREAK

Don't leave Monte Carlo without treating yourself to the comparatively inexpensive pleasure of sipping a cup of coffee in one of the cafés around Place du Casino, on the terrace of the Café de Paris or in the Métropole shopping centre, while watching the comings and goings of Monaco's beautiful people. Also consider treating yourself to a superb lunch in any of the top hotels; it won't be cheap but it's a less expensive way than dinner to experience the very best of Monaco's haute cuisine.

Bar-Tabacs des Moulins £ ❶ It's tiny but somehow always manages to fit everyone in, the service is quick, and the food fresh and inexpensive. ❸ 46 blvd des Moulins ❶ 93 50 66 39 🕐 10.00–21.00 Mon–Sat ❷ Bus: 1, 4 to Place des Moulins

Häagen Dazs £ ❷ This famous ice cream chain has the perfect spot near Place du Casino. ❸ Av de la Princesse Alice ❶ 93 30 38 30 🕐 10.00–22.00 daily (until 23.00 June & July) ❷ Bus: 1, 2, 4, 6 to Casino Tourisme

MetCafé £–££ ❸ This swanky bar and café offers gourmet snacks and sandwiches on the ground floor of the Métropole shopping gallery. ❸ Centre Commercial Le Métropole, 17 av des Spélugues ❶ 93 15 13 79 🕐 10.00–19.30 Mon–Sat ❷ Bus: 1, 6 to Place du Casino

La Note Bleue £–££ ❹ Great daytime café and bar, perfect for lunch in between sunbathing sessions on Larvotto's beach (for which you can rent a deckchair here). Tapas and live music by the sea. ❸ Plage du Larvotto ❶ 93 50 05 02 🔵 www.lanotebleue.mc 🕐 08.00–18.00 daily (until 22.30 mid-May–mid-Sept); closed mid-Dec–mid-Mar ❷ Bus: 6 to Plages

La Vigie ££ ❺ This upmarket brasserie at the SBM-owned Monte Carlo Beach Hotel is technically not in Monte Carlo or even in Monaco, and it's certainly not a low-cost option, but if you like a really good Sunday brunch it's the place to go (the in-crowd usually arrive by yacht). ❸ Av Princesse Grace, Roquebrune-Cap-Martin ☎ 98 06 52 52 🌐 www.montecarlobeachhotel.com 🕐 Lunch & dinner Tues–Sun (times vary) 🚗 Take a taxi – or hire a yacht!

AFTER DARK

RESTAURANTS

The relatively tiny area of Monte Carlo probably has more restaurants than most big European cities, so any selection is just the tip of the iceberg, and there are plenty more than this to discover. Though the area is not given over entirely to haute cuisine, that's what it's best known for.

La Spiaggia £ ❻ Right on Larvotto beach, this cheap but cheerful eatery attracts both locals and tourists for a spot of lunch in the sun, or a game of table tennis or backgammon. ❸ Av Princesse Grace ☎ 93 50 50 80 🕐 09.00–24.00 daily 🚌 Bus: 6 to Larvotto

Cosmopolitan £–££ ❼ With a truly cosmopolitan menu and an extensive list of wines from around the world, this place caters well to the varied tastes of Monte Carlo's multinational visitors. ❸ 7 rue du Portier ☎ 93 25 78 68 🌐 www.cosmopolitan.mc 🕐 12.30–14.00, 19.30–23.00 Mon–Fri 🚌 Bus: 6 to Larvotto

Rampoldi Restaurant ££ ❽ Affordable eating, given the area, with Italian specialities, in this long-established restaurant. ❸ 2 av des Spélugues ☎ 93 30 70 65 🕐 12.00–14.30, 19.30–23.30 daily 🚌 Bus: 1, 2, 4, 6 to Casino Tourisme

Il Terrazzino ££ ❾ Authentic southern-Italian cooking, especially good on antipasti and pasta, and the generous portions make this a good-value stop for a full lunch or dinner. A couple of blocks back from the Casino. ❷ 2 rue des Iris ❶ 93 50 24 27 Ⓦ www.il-terrazzino.com ◔ 12.00–14.30, 19.30–23.00 daily Ⓝ Bus: 1, 2, 4, 6 to Casino Tourisme

Café de Paris ££–£££ ❿ Dining at the Café de Paris, right on Place du Casino, is a date with history. It numbers the great Escoffier among its former chefs – this is the kitchen in which he accidentally invented *crêpes suzettes* in 1898. Not that there's anything stuffy or old-fashioned about the food in this stylish brasserie, which does excellent cocktails and from time to time offers special menus on themes such as Provençal or Latin American cuisine. ❷ Pl du Casino ❶ 98 06 76 23 Ⓝ Bus: 1, 2, 4, 6 to Casino Tourisme

Pacific ££–£££ ⓫ Pacific is the ultra-hip brainchild of the former manager of the glamorous Jimmy'z nightclub, and one of the places to see and be seen in Monaco. The food is an elegant fusion of Japanese and Italian. ❷ 17 av des Spélugues ❶ 93 25 20 30 ◔ 12.00–15.00, 19.30–24.00 daily Ⓝ Bus: 1, 2, 4, 6 to Casino Tourisme

Joël Robuchon £££ ⓬ This Michelin-starred restaurant is the Hôtel Métropole's crowning glory. Named after its famous chef, it is currently hot on the heels of the Louis XV for the title of best restaurant in the Principality. ❸ Hôtel Métropole, 4 av de la Madone ❶ 93 15 15 10 Ⓦ www.joel-robuchon.com ◔ 12.15–14.30, 19.30–22.30 daily Ⓝ Bus: 1, 2, 4, 6 to Casino Tourisme

Louis XV £££ ⓭ The renowned restaurant of the Hôtel de Paris has one of the most glamorous terraces in the world and a dining room decorated in the style of Versailles. This is Alain Ducasse's flagship restaurant, though the *chef de cuisine* is now Franck Cerutti. You won't come across many better dining experiences, provided your wallet can take it (let the menu on the website tempt you). ⓐ Hôtel de Paris, Pl du Casino ⓣ 98 06 88 64 ⓦ www.alain-ducasse.com ⓛ 12.15–13.45, 20.00–21.45 Thur–Mon ⓝ Bus: 1, 2, 4, 6 to Casino Tourisme

Yoshi £££ ⓮ Chef Takeo Yamazaki aims to meet the expectations of lovers of healthy modern Japanese cuisine in this classy restaurant with restful Zen decoration which forms part of the Hôtel Métropole. It has a sushi bar and a beautiful garden. ⓐ Hôtel Métropole, 4 av de la Madone ⓣ 93 15 13 13 ⓛ 12.15–14.00, 19.30–22.30 Tues–Sun

BARS & CLUBS
Buddha Bar This charming and spacious bar, where you can have dinner or just a drink, is one the trendiest places in town. It is located at the east wing of the Casino, with a gigantic statue of Buddha presiding over the customers. The careful lighting, Chinese and Japanese sculptures, and rich colours of the materials and wood panels make it an atmospheric place to escape the urban mayhem. ⓐ Pl du Casino ⓣ 98 06 36 36 ⓦ www.buddha-bar.com

Jimmy'z The legendary nightclub and disco at the Sporting d'Eté attracts models, pop stars, and the rich and famous in general, so be prepared to dress the part and pay the prices. ⓐ 26 av Princesse Grace ⓣ 98 06 70 61 (before 23.00); 98 06 70 68 (after 23.00) ⓦ www.montecarloresort.com ⓛ 23.30–dawn Wed–Sun ⓝ Bus: 6 to Carmes

McCarthy's Pub Not all of Monte Carlo is exclusive and image-obsessed, and McCarthy's provides the friendly and lively atmosphere of a typical Irish bar, with live music, a DJ and all the Guinness® you can drink. Locals happily mix with the occasional celebrity seeking refuge from the glitz. ❷ 7 rue du Portier ❶ 93 50 88 10 ❸ 17.00–dawn daily ❽ Bus: 6 to Portier

Sabor di Vino This cosy bar's passion for wine is infectious, and they even bring you a free platter of tasty delicacies to help bring out your wine's subtler flavours. ❷ Galerie Charles III, corner Av des

THE MAN WHO BROKE THE BANK AT MONTE CARLO

A popular British music-hall song of 1892 with this title was inspired by the exploits of English gambler Charles Wells. But it was his fellow countryman Joseph Jagger who really did break the bank at Monte Carlo, 20 years earlier. An engineer in the mills of Victorian Yorkshire, he arrived in Monte Carlo in 1873 determined to prove that roulette wheels, being just machines, could be beaten. After compiling a mass of statistics on the roll of the wheels, he identified nine numbers that regularly came up on one of the six wheels in use at the Casino owing to a slight imbalance in its mechanism. He proceeded to bet heavily on them and on his first night cleared nearly £14,000. The Casino switched wheels between tables overnight but he soon identified the imperfect one and continued to win. Eventually he won over £65,000, making him a multi-millionaire in today's money. Sadly, he died in the year the song came out.

Spélugues & Av de la Madone ☏ 99 99 98 00 🕓 18.00–dawn daily
Ⓝ Bus: 1, 2, 6 to Ostende or Ostende Supérieur

Zelos Sophisticated bar on the top floor of the Grimaldi Forum with
a dancing area. Enjoy a cocktail under the stars on the fantastic
terrace. ⓐ Grimaldi Forum, 10 av Princesse Grace ☏ 99 99 25 50
🕓 11.00–02.30 daily Ⓝ Bus: 6 to Larvotto

CASINOS

Monte Carlo is where Monaco's nightlife begins and ends. You can mix
with the glamorous crowd at the Casino and other fashionable
hangouts for the price of a drink, though to feel really comfortable
you'll want to wear your smartest evening wear – casual is fine (except
at the Casino) but make it very chic-casual if you hope to blend in.

Remember, whatever your intentions, if you want to play at a
casino you need to be over 21 and have your passport or national
identity card with you. Minimum dress code for gentlemen is a
sports jacket and tie. There's no specific code for ladies, but it might
be worth observing arrivals the night before to check out what the
competition is wearing. If you're a roulette novice, see page 31 for
the different styles; you can download full rules from the Casino
website (see page 65).

Café de Paris American roulette, craps, blackjack, slot machines and
video poker in the venerable Café's three gaming rooms. ⓐ Pl du
Casino ☏ 98 06 77 77 🆆 www.montecarlocasinos.com 🕓 From 10.00
(slots); 16.00 (video poker); 17.00 (roulette and card tables)

Casino d'Eté Part of the legendary Sporting d'Eté, this summer casino
juts out on its own promontory facing Larvotto beach and is always

in fashion. Dine, sip cocktails, dance till dawn, enjoy acts from world-famous stars, or lose your shirt at the roulette tables – it's your choice and they're not mutually exclusive options either. You could pack the equivalent of two very full nights out into one evening here. ⓐ 26 av Princesse Grace ⓣ 98 06 72 00 ⓦ www.montecarlocasinos.com ⓛ From 22.00 (July & Aug only) ⓦ Bus: 6 to Larvotto

Casino de Monte-Carlo The Casino is divided into differently styled rooms, all with admission charges of €10–20 per person. Slot machines are in the Salle Blanche (white room), French and English roulette and *trente et quarante* can be found in the Salle Europe (European room), and craps and blackjack in the Salle des Amériques (American room). The Salons Privés (private rooms) offer English and European roulette, *chemin de fer* and other more abstruse games, but for high rollers only. ⓐ Pl du Casino ⓣ 98 06 21 21 ⓦ www.montecarlo casinos.com ⓛ Salle Blanche: from 14.00 Mon–Fri, from 12.00 Sat & Sun. Salles Europe & des Amériques: from 12.00 daily. Consult the casino website for more detail ⓦ Bus: 1, 2, 4, 6 to Casino Tourisme. Arrival by taxi or hired limo is more the done thing, however.

Salle des Palmiers is part of the Casino d'Eté (see page 75) and is the only gaming room with a sea view. The same games are played here as at the Casino de Monte-Carlo, with the addition of American roulette.

Sun Casino Once owned by an independent hotel, the Sun Casino has since merged with the great SBM monopoly, even though the hotel it's housed in hasn't. Its collection of slot machines is 435 strong and you'll find craps and blackjack as well as American roulette tables (see page 31). ⓐ Fairmont Monte Carlo Hotel, 12 av des

Spélugues ☎ 98 06 12 12 ⓦ www.montecarlocasinos.com 🕐 From
12.00 (slots); 17.00 Mon–Fri, 16.00 Sat & Sun (tables)

SHOWS & ENTERTAINMENT

In the winter season, you can enjoy classic and contemporary
opera productions in the Salle Garnier, part of the Casino and Opéra
complex (see page 64), and at the Grimaldi Forum (see page 65).
At any time of year it's worth checking with the tourist office to
see what in the way of pop and orchestral concerts is taking place at
the Grimaldi Forum and other Monte Carlo venues.

Le Moods Live music ranging from a Ray Charles cover band to the
hippest of jazz and blues artists. There is a tasty tapas selection and
an extensive wine list. ⓐ Pl du Casino ☎ 98 06 20 08 🕐 19.00–02.00
Tues–Sat (event hours vary – call to check)

Salle des Etoiles Located in the Sporting d'Eté club, the Salle des
Etoiles is the most prestigious concert venue in Monaco and showcases
world-renowned talent every night during the summer. When the
event is advertised as a Gala Evening, it means it's a special event
in aid of charity and everyone who is anyone in Monaco will be
there. The dress code steps up a notch on these occasions, too. Gala
Evening or not, it's worth splashing out: tickets are expensive but the
shows are unique, with a three-course meal and fireworks to finish.
ⓐ 26 av Princesse Grace ☎ 98 06 72 72 ⓦ www.montecarloresort.com
🕐 Event times vary but usually 20.30 for dinner, 22.45 for the show
(July & Aug only) ⓝ Bus: 6 to Larvotto

Monaco-Ville

This most conservative of the districts of Monaco is the home of the reigning family and most of the oldest-established Monégasque families. Its 86-m (280-ft)-high rocky outcrop was the site of the old Ghibelline castle (now replaced by the Palais Princier – see page 81), where the first Grimaldi ruler founded his family's 700-year reign. The layout is medieval, with narrow streets and alleys opening on to small squares and fountains. It is the cultural and religious heart of Monaco, and the traditional Provençal architecture of the buildings and Catholic churches reflects this.

SIGHTS & ATTRACTIONS

Cathédrale de Monaco

Leaving Place du Palais at its southern end by Rue Colonel Bellando de Castro, it's a short walk to Monaco's cathedral. Built in 1875, like much of modern Monaco in white stone from nearby La Turbie, the neo-Romanesque cathedral stands on the site of a 13th-century chapel of St Nicholas. Here, among the tombs of other Grimaldi princes and princesses, you will find the simple slab that marks the tomb of Princess Grace. The Cathedral is also noteworthy for its altarpiece of St Nicholas, the work of Louis Bréa in 1500, and the impressive modern four-keyboard organ. ❸ 4 rue Col Bellando de Castro ❶ 93 30 87 70 ❺ 08.30–19.00 daily (summer); 08.30–18.45 daily (winter) ❿ www.cathedrale.mc ❻ Bus: 1, 2 to Monaco Ville

Chapelle de la Miséricorde (Chapel of Mercy)

Built in 1639, the chapel was founded by the Order of Black Penitents. It houses a collection of religious art, including a wooden sculpture

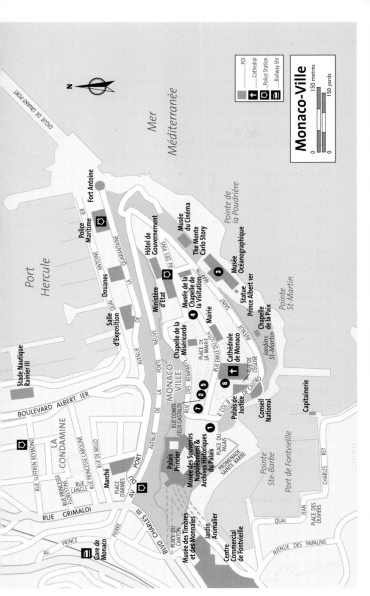

Monaco-Ville

POI
Cathedral
Police Station
Railway Stn

0 ————— 150 metres
0 ————— 150 yards

N

Port Hercule

Mer Méditerranée

DIGUE DE L'AVANT-PORT

Stade Nautique Rainier III

BOULEVARD ALBERT IER

LA CONDAMINE

RUE SUFFREN REYMOND
RUE PRINCESSE FLORESTINE
RUE PRINCESSE CAROLINE
RUE DE MILLO
RUE LANGLE

RUE GRIMALDI

AV. PRINCE PIERRE

Gare de Monaco

Marché

PLACE D'ARMES

BLVD CHARLES III

AV. DU PORT

PLACE DU CANTON

Palais Princier

Musée des Souvenirs Napoléoniens & Archives Historiques du Palais

Musée des Timbres et des Monnaies

Jardin Animalier

Centre Commercial de Fontvieille

AVENUE DES PAPALINS

QUAI JEAN CHARLES REY

PLACE DES OLIVIERS

Pointe Ste-Barbe

Port de Fontvieille

Capitainerie

Conseil National

Palais de Justice

PROMENADE SAINTE BARBE

PLACE DU PALAIS

RUE COL. B

R. COL B

RUE COMTE FÉLIX GASTALDI

MONACO-VILLE

RUE DES REMPARTS

RUE EMILE DUCLOUX

RUE DE L'ÉGLISE

DE CASTRO

PLACE DE LA MAIRIE

Cathédrale de Monaco

Chapelle de la Miséricorde

Mairie

Musée de la Chapelle de la Visitation

Jardins St-Martin

Chapelle de la Paix

Statue Prince Albert Ier

AVENUE SAINT MARTIN

Pointe St-Martin

Pointe de la Poudrière

Musée Océanographique

The Monte Carlo Story

Musée du Cinéma

Hôtel de Gouvernement

Ministère d'État

AV. DES PINS

AVENUE DE LA PORTE NEUVE

Salle d'Exposition

QUAI ANTOINE IER

DE LA QUARANTAINE

Douanes

Police Maritime

Fort Antoine

1
2
5
6
7
4
3

of Christ by François-Joseph Bosio, the Monaco-born official sculptor to the Emperor Napoléon I. ❸ Pl de la Mairie 🕐 10.00–18.00 daily 🅝 Bus: 1, 2 to Monaco Ville

Chapelle de la Paix (Chapel of Peace)

Within the Jardins St-Martin stands this tiny white chapel, the resting place of Prince Pierre, father of the late Prince Rainier, and Stefano Casiraghi, the second husband of Princess Caroline, who was killed in 1990 in a speedboat accident while defending his World Offshore title. 🅝 Bus: 1, 2 to Monaco Ville

Fort Antoine

This early 18th-century fortress stands on the very end of the Rock of Monaco. It is now used as an open-air theatre with a capacity of 350 spectators in tiered semicircular seating – an atmospheric setting for evening performances during the summer. ❸ Av de la Quarantaine ☎ 98 98 83 03 🕐 24 hrs except during performances 🅝 Bus: 1, 2 to Monaco Ville

Jardins St-Martin (St Martin's Gardens)

Facing the Cathedral is the western end of the long garden that overlooks Fontvieille harbour. This 19th-century park of Aleppo pines and exotic plants was a favourite haunt of the poet Apollinaire. It is decorated with bronze statues, including a modern one of Prince Albert I, the guiding spirit behind the Oceanographic Institute, whose museum is located nearby (see page 84).

The Monte Carlo Story

This is the history of the Principality and its development into one of the world's leading pleasure capitals, told in a 30-minute film with simultaneous translation into English and five other languages. There is also a small museum of cinema posters of films that have featured Monte Carlo as a backdrop. ❷ Terrasses du Parking des Pêcheurs, off Av St-Martin ❶ 93 25 32 33 Ⓦ www.monaco-memory.com ❶ 14.00–17.00 daily (Jan–June & Sept–Nov); 14.00–18.00 daily (July & Aug) Ⓑ Bus: 1, 2 to Monaco Ville ❶ Admission charge

Palais Princier (Prince's Palace)

Built on the site of the 13th-century castle of François Grimaldi, the Palais has been extended several times, particularly during the Renaissance. At its heart is an immense square, the Cour d'Honneur, paved with three million coloured pebbles in immense geometric patterns; concerts are held here during the summer. Dominating the Cour is an imposing 17th-century horseshoe-shaped double staircase made of Carrara marble. Behind the staircase is the Galerie

🔺 *The distinctive white-stone Cathédrale de Monaco*

à l'Italienne, a long gallery linking the state apartments, decorated with 16th-century Genoese frescoes of mythological scenes. These include the yellow and gold Louis XV Salon, the blue and gold Salon Bleu, and the Mazarin Salon, decorated with coloured wooden panels. The real highlight, however, is the impressive Salon du Trône (Throne Room) and its Renaissance fireplace. Audio-guided tours of the Palace, available whenever the Prince is not in residence, take in all of these sights. One wing of the palace houses the state archives and the Musée des Souvenirs Napoléoniens (see opposite). The Sainte-Marie Tower is a more modern addition, built by Albert I in the early 20th century; this is where the Prince's red-and-white standard is flown when he is in residence. ❸ Pl du Palais ❶ 93 25 18 31 ⓦ www.palais.mc ❶ 10.00–18.00 daily (Apr–Oct) ⓝ Bus: 1, 2 to Monaco Ville ❶ Admission charge for 30-min tour

Le Petit Train (part of the Azur Express)

This little red-and-white train takes you on a short tour around Monaco. Aside from being the most adorable thing in town, it also conducts a half-hour trip around the main areas of touristic interest in the Principality. It goes slowly, giving everyone a chance to enjoy the sights and the sun on the way. ❸ Departure and arrivals outside the Musée Océanographique (see page 84) ❶ 92 05 64 38 ⓦ www.monacotours.mc ❶ 10.00–17.00 daily (summer); 10.30–17.00 daily (winter) ⓝ Bus: 1, 2 to Monaco Ville ❶ Admission charge

Place du Palais (Palace Square)

The large square in front of the Palais Princier is lined with bronze cannons, a thoughtful gift from Monaco's ally Louis XIV of France. The panoramas from all sides of the square offer views as far as

Italy. At 11.55 every day the Prince's guard of *carabiniers* (uniformed in black during the winter, white in summer) perform the 100-year-old ceremony of the Changing of the Guard in front of the Palace. Their barracks face the palace across the square.

The square is connected to the lower-level town via the red-brick-paved Rampe Major and its two gates, all dating from the 16th century, which until the 19th century was the only means of approach from Condamine. ⊘ Bus: 1, 2 to Monaco Ville

CULTURE

Musée de la Chapelle de la Visitation

The Baroque 17th-century Chapelle de la Visitation, a short walk north from the Musée Océanographique, houses a remarkable, privately assembled collection of religious art, including works by Rubens and Italian masters of the Baroque period. ❸ Pl de la Visitation, at end of Av des Pins ☎ 93 50 07 00 🕐 10.00–16.00 Tues–Sun ⊘ Bus: 1, 2 to Monaco Ville ❶ Admission charge

Musée des Souvenirs Napoléoniens & Archives Historiques du Palais (Napoleonic Museum & Historic Archives of the Palace)

Two museums in one, housed in the south wing of the Palais Princier. The ground floor is the Napoleonic Museum, with a collection of more than 1,000 objects and documents relating to, or once owned by, Emperor Napoleon I. Considering Napoleon's rough treatment of the House of Grimaldi (see page 14), it seems quite generous of them to make space in their home for what is one of the finest collections of Napoleonic memorabilia in Europe.

The first floor of the wing is dedicated to the history of the Principality. Exhibits include the medieval Charter of Independence of Monaco, a letter written by Louis XIV to Prince Antoine I, uniforms of the Prince's Guards, and medals bestowed by and upon the princes of Monaco. ⓐ Pl du Palais ⓣ 93 25 18 31 ⓦ www.palais.mc ⓛ 10.30–17.00 daily (Jan–Mar & Dec); 10.00–18.00 daily (Apr–Oct); closed Nov ⓝ Bus: 1, 2 to Monaco Ville ⓘ Admission charge

Musée Océanographique (Oceanographic Museum)

Perched on a cliff overlooking the sea, the Oceanographic Institute boasts a world-class museum that is a fascinating excursion for adults and children alike. Born out of the passion two of Monaco's former princes held for the sea, the museum has grown into an impressive collection of rare marine specimens and antique sea-exploration devices.

On the top floor you can have lunch in the café (see page 87) while admiring the magnificent views of Monaco and the Italian Riviera; there is also a good museum shop.

Once you've visited the museum, consider taking the quaint touristic train (see page 82) that stops outside just for a guided tour back into Monte Carlo. ⓐ Av St-Martin ⓣ 93 15 36 00 ⓦ www.oceano.org ⓛ 09.30–19.00 daily (Apr–June & Sept); 09.30–19.30 daily (July & Aug); 10.00–18.00 daily (Oct & Dec–Mar); closed Nov ⓝ Bus: 1, 2 to Monaco Ville ⓘ Admission charge

RETAIL THERAPY

There are literally dozens of souvenir and gift shops squeezed into the narrow streets of Monaco-Ville. They all offer similar wares, including handicrafts and fun jewellery, and it pays to browse before buying, as the further away from the tourist epicentres (especially in the Palais Princier) you stroll, the more

○ *What better setting for a marine research institute?*

affordable the prices are likely to be. Perhaps the best places to find authentic Monégasque handicrafts and products are the Boutique du Rocher and Ombre & Soleil.

Boutique du Rocher ② 11 rue Emile de Loth ① 93 30 33 99
① 10.30–18.00 Mon, Tues, Thur & Fri

Ombre & Soleil ② 29 rue Comte Felix Gastaldi, off Pl du Palais, 2nd right after Rue des Remparts ① 93 50 07 15 ① 10.00–19.00 daily

Poco This shop sells a variety of works of art and paintings, as well as jewellery and fashion accessories. ② 6 rue Princesse Marie de Lorraine ① 93 30 99 99 ① 10.00–19.00 daily

TAKING A BREAK

Le Castelroc £ ❶ A traditional café/restaurant in a prime position, Le Castelroc is very convenient for a coffee break or lunch after visiting the Palace. Local dishes are a speciality – try a traditional *barbajuan* (see page 29). ② Pl du Palais ① 93 30 36 68 ① 09.00–17.00 Mon, Fri & Sun, 09.00–19.30 Tues–Thur ② Bus: 1, 2 to Monaco Ville

Crêperie du Rocher £ ❷ There's nothing better for a light lunch than a savoury pancake or a pizza, and this *crêperie* on a side street off Place du Palais specialises in both. ② 12 rue Comte Félix Gastaldi, off Pl du Palais ① 93 30 09 64 ① 11.00–23.00 Tues–Sat (Sept–June); 11.00–23.00 daily (July & Aug) ② Bus: 1, 2 to Monaco Ville

Terrasse du Musée £ ❸ The café at the top of the Musée Océanographique (see page 84) is a great place to enjoy sea views

with a drink or spot of lunch. ⓐ Av St-Martin ⓣ 93 15 36 00
ⓛ 09.30–19.00 Tues–Sun (Apr–Sept); 10.00–18.00 Tues–Sun
(Oct–Mar) ⓦ Bus: 1, 2 to Monaco Ville

Chocolaterie de Monaco ££ ❹ Enjoy tea fit for a king – or a prince –
at this tea room, home of the prince's official chocolate suppliers.
ⓐ Pl de la Visitation, at end of Av des Pins ⓣ 97 97 88 88 ⓛ 09.30–
18.30 Mon–Sat ⓦ Bus: 1, 2 to Monaco Ville

AFTER DARK

Monaco-Ville is a district of small, generally family-run restaurants –
only a limited number of which stay open in the evenings.

RESTAURANTS

Pasta Roca £ ❺ A good selection of pizzas, crêpes, and local and
regional specialities. ⓐ 23 rue Comte Félix Gastaldi, off Pl du Palais
ⓣ 93 50 07 15 or 93 30 44 22 ⓛ 09.00–15.00, 18.30–22.00 daily
ⓦ Bus: 1, 2 to Monaco Ville

Saint-Nicolas £ ❻ The quiet location near the cathedral and a
good selection of traditional Monégasque and Provençal dishes
make this a popular choice, daytime or evening. ⓐ 6 rue de
l'Eglise ⓣ 93 30 30 41 ⓛ 12.00–15.00, 19.00–22.30 daily ⓦ Bus: 1, 2
to Monaco Ville

Le Pinocchio £–££ ❼ This longstanding traditional Italian
restaurant is in a great spot just off Place du Palais. ⓐ 30 rue Comte
Félix Gastaldi ⓣ 93 30 96 20 ⓛ 12.00–15.00, 19.30–24.00 daily
ⓦ Bus: 1, 2 to Monaco Ville

● *Monaco-Ville is the city's best area for traditional bistros*

ENTERTAINMENT

With all the nightlife of Monte Carlo only a few hundred metres away, not many visitors or locals choose to make Monaco-Ville their night-time destination. However, it does possess two noteworthy attractions, both open-air and summer only, and both near the tip of the promontory: the **Cinéma d'Eté** on top of the Pêcheurs car park (see page 31), and the theatre at **Fort Antoine** (see page 80), a converted 18th-century fortress that holds up to 350 spectators in a tiered semicircle, providing a magical setting for drama and music events.

La Condamine & Moneghetti

La Condamine, once the vegetable gardens of the Palais Princier, is the most bustling and down-to-earth area of Monaco; a district of busy shopping streets and small hotels hemmed in between the main railway line and the harbour. Moneghetti, beyond the railway and backing on to the mountains, is quieter, but has one or two worthwhile attractions.

SIGHTS & ATTRACTIONS

Eglise Ste-Dévote (St Dévote's Church)

This 19th-century chapel replaced a medieval oratory built on the spot where a ship carrying the remains of St Dévote, a Corsican martyr, supposedly ran aground after a storm in the 4th century AD. She became the patron saint of Monaco. According to another legend a thief tried to make off with her relics when they turned out to have miraculous powers, but he was caught by local fishermen, who burnt his boat. At dusk on 26 January, the eve of the saint's day, a boat is burnt in commemoration, following a torchlight procession to the chapel. ❸ Pl Ste-Dévote ☎ 93 50 52 60 ⏱ 08.30–18.00 daily Ⓝ Bus: 1, 2, 5, 6 to Place Ste-Dévote

Jardin Exotique, Grotte de l'Observatoire & Musée d'Anthropologie Préhistorique

One of Monaco's most popular attractions is the **Jardin Exotique (Exotic Garden)**, a dry garden created on a rock face in Moneghetti in 1933 containing thousands of weird and wonderful cacti and other succulents from all over the world, which thrive in the area's microclimate. It is more colourful than it sounds, since many of

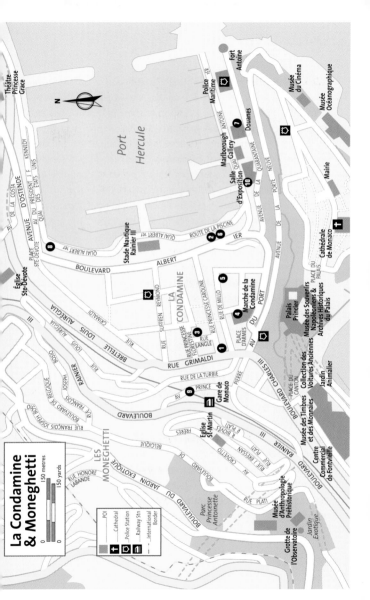

these plants have impressive blooms that flower at different times, creating year-round interest. The garden is an important international centre for the study and propagation of these plants. There is also a snack bar and a shop selling cacti.

Part of the same complex as the Jardin Exotique, the name of the **Grotte de l'Observatoire (Observatory Cave)** is slightly misleading, as it has nothing to do with stargazing. Opened to the public in 1950, it is a natural cavern, some 60 m (200 ft) below the Jardin Exotique, once occupied by Stone Age man and now filled with impressive stalagmites and stalactites. The full tour lasts a good two hours.

The Riviera region was a favourite dwelling site for prehistoric man, as evidenced in the nearby cave. The **Musée d'Anthropologie Préhistorique (Museum of Prehistoric Anthropology)** displays the remains of mankind's occupation over the last million years, including exhibits charting the human race's progress from Australopithecus to Homo sapiens, and many extinct animals. ⓐ 62 blvd du Jardin Exotique ⓣ 93 15 29 80 ⓦ www.jardin-exotique.mc ⓛ All attractions: 09.00–19.00 daily (mid-May–mid-Sept); 09.00–18.00 daily (mid-Sept–mid-May) ⓝ Bus: 2 to Jardin Exotique ⓘ One admission charge covers the garden, cave and museum.

Marlborough Gallery

Founded in London in 1946, the commercial Marlborough Gallery opened its Monaco outpost in 2000 in a converted warehouse near the port. As well as staging an ever-changing series of exhibitions of contemporary and modern classic artists, it also represents some of the best-known names in modern art. ⓐ 4 quai Antoine 1er ⓣ 97 70 25 50 ⓦ www.marlborough-monaco.com ⓛ 11.00–18.00 Mon–Fri ⓝ Bus: 1, 2, 5, 6 to Princesse Stéphanie

Parc Princesse Antoinette

This delightful open space was purchased in 1916 by Prince Albert I,
who was concerned to preserve the last remaining natural areas of
his Principality from development. It was, and still is, an olive grove.
There were 156 trees left at the time of purchase, to which the late
Prince Rainier and his son Albert added a 157th in 1993 to commemorate
Monaco joining the United Nations. As well as olive trees, the park
contains flowerbeds and streams crossed by little bridges, making
it a welcome refuge from the urban side of Monaco. Under Prince
Louis II in the 1920s, the park was dedicated to the children of Monaco,
and was named after his daughter Antoinette. There is also a
playground and a mini-golf course for children. On the western edge
of the park is one of the two sites of the Nouveau Musée National
de Monaco, the Villa Paloma (see page 66). The park is traditionally
visited once a year on the last Sunday of June by the reigning
monarch and most of the Monégasque population for a giant
family picnic. **⊘** 54 bis blvd du Jardin Exotique **❶** 93 30 92 12
◷ 08.30–sunset daily **⊗** Bus: 2 to Hector Otto **❶** Admission to park
free; small admission charge to playground

Place d'Armes

One side of this large square is dominated by the Condamine fruit
and vegetable market. Sitting under the Rocher (or Rock) of Monaco,
it is a natural meeting place for citizens and tourists, with plenty
of pavement cafés, newsstands and other everyday conveniences.
There's also a children's play area. **⊗** Bus: 1, 2, 4, 5, 6 to Place d'Armes

Port Hercule

The main harbour, also known as Port de Monaco, is where you'll
find Monaco's most luxurious yachts, a succession of cruise ships

93

and Monaco's newest project – the Digue, a floating jetty. The centre of the quayside is dominated by the Olympic-size swimming pool at the Stade Nautique Rainier III (see below). The Port is also known for its themed fairs, notably its annual Christmas Village (see opposite).

🚍 Bus: 1, 2, 5, 6 to Princesse Stéphanie

Stade Nautique Rainier III

There's no need to go out to the beach at Larvotto if you fancy a swim. This watersports stadium, with an open-air Olympic-size swimming pool, sits in the very middle of Monaco, perched over the harbour, with great views of the town and the mountains as a bonus. The 1,250-sq m (12,000-sq ft) pool is filled with 3,000 cu m (100,000 cu ft) of treated seawater kept at 26°C (79°F). You can pay as you go in or buy books of tickets (*carnets*) for repeat visits, and mats and parasols can be hired. From December to March it serves instead as Monaco's

🔺 *Port Hercule bustles with life as night falls*

CHRISTMAS VILLAGE
Every year from the beginning of December, the quay overlooking the port is transformed into a winter wonderland complete with tiny chalets, activities for young and old, entertainers, and oyster and champagne stands – based on a different theme each year. The success of the Christmas Village is paving the way for additional events throughout the year, so watch this space. ⓐ Quai Albert 1er ⓣ 93 15 06 02 ⓦ www.monaco-mairie.mc ⓝ Bus: 1, 2, 5, 6 to Stade Nautique

ice rink. ⓐ Quai Albert 1er ⓣ 93 30 64 83 ⓛ 09.00–18.00 Tues–Sun (May–Oct) ⓝ Bus: 1, 2, 5, 6 to Stade Nautique ⓘ Admission charge

RETAIL THERAPY

If you're shopping for everyday items, or looking for gifts and fashion accessories that bit more affordable than what Monte Carlo has to offer, make for La Condamine. For anything nautical, head for the quaysides of Port Hercule and their surrounding streets. For fresh produce and a cheerful atmosphere, choose the big central market. For all other shopping, you need look no further than Rue Princesse Caroline, the nearby Rue Grimaldi and, behind it, Rue de la Turbie.

Le Marché de la Condamine Monaco's main market has plenty to offer in spite of the rather functional appearance of the building itself. The exterior is dominated by a flower market; inside you'll find many food stalls – bakers, butchers, *charcutiers* – offering Monégasque specialities. If you're planning a picnic, this should be your first stop. It's also a social centre, with a couple of welcoming and agreeable bars, and is the best place to observe the everyday life of Monaco away from the glitz and millionaire ambience. ❸ Pl d'Armes Ⓝ Bus: 1, 2, 4, 5, 6 to Place d'Armes

Boutique Formule 1 Everything to do with the world of F1 is available here, including clothes, miniature cars, watches, books, perfumes and other paraphernalia. ❷ 15 rue Grimaldi ❶ 93 15 92 44 ❷ 10.00–13.00, 14.00–19.00 daily (spring & summer); 10.00–12.30, 14.30–18.30 daily (autumn & winter)

TAKING A BREAK

Bar de Monaco £ ❶ The name suggests that the whole Principality heads to this busy marketplace bar, and sometimes that seems not far short of the truth. Lots of local life. ❷ 1 pl d'Armes ❶ 93 30 12 58 ❷ 07.00–20.00 Tues–Sun Ⓝ Bus: 1, 2, 4, 5, 6 to Place d'Armes

Brasserie de Monaco £ ❷ This bar and brewery in Port Hercule is a great place for a quick snack or aperitif. There are several big screens for sporting events, and a room for dancing opens up later in the evening. ❷ 30 route de la Piscine, Port Hercule ❶ 97 98 51 20 Ⓦ www.brasseriedemonaco.com ❷ 11.00–01.00 Mon–Fri, 11.00–03.00 Sat & Sun Ⓝ Bus: 1, 2, 4, 5, 6 to Place d'Armes

Le Huit et Demi £–££ ❸ An excellent and terribly popular eatery, Le Huit et Demi enjoys a loyal fan base. The cooking contains plenty of fresh ingredients from the day's market. ❷ 4 rue Langlé ❶ 93 50 97 02 ❷ 12.00–23.00 daily Ⓝ Bus: 1, 2, 4, 5, 6 to Place d'Armes

○ *Le Marché de la Condamine spills out into Place d'Armes*

Le Zinc £–££ ❹ This busy bar in the heart of the covered market has bags of atmosphere and is one place where you can be sure of mixing with the locals. ❸ Marché de la Condamine, Pl d'Armes ❶ 93 50 93 99 ❺ 05.30–13.30 Mon–Sat ❷ Bus: 1, 2, 4, 5, 6 to Place d'Armes

AFTER DARK

RESTAURANTS
Royal Thai £ ❺ Satisfying spicy dishes, including some great vegetarian treats – unusual for meat-loving Monaco. Great for lunch or dinner. ❸ 18 rue de Millo ❶ 93 30 16 14 ❺ 12.00–15.00, 18.30–23.00 daily ❷ Buses: 1, 2, 5, 6 to Stade Nautique

PizzArt £–££ ❻ Classic pizza and other staples of Italian cuisine. The chic décor – half Baroque, half modern – draws a trendy crowd, as does the live music at weekends. ❸ 32 route de la Piscine, Port Hercule ❶ 97 98 34 56 ❿ www.pizzart.mc ❺ 11.00–01.00 daily ❷ Bus: 1, 2 5, 6 to Place d'Armes

Stars'N'Bars £–££ ❼ This three-storey bar, restaurant and entertainment complex overlooking the harbour (and the paddocks during Grand Prix weekend) is as much a favourite with tourists as with celebrity customers, who include some of the best known names in Formula 1 racing. The food style is predominantly American and Tex-Mex. Among its other attractions are a cybercafé, a children's room and an upstairs club with live bands. ❸ 6 quai Antoine 1er ❶ 97 97 95 95 ❿ www.starsnbars.com ❺ 09.30–01.00 Tues–Sun (kitchen 11.00–24.00); also open Mon in summer ❷ Bus: 1, 2, 4, 5, 6 to Place d'Armes

Tender to... £–££ ❽ This modern restaurant replaced the
much-loved Restaurant du Port but is already proving a hit with
its modern takes on classic Mediterranean dishes. ⓐ Quai Albert 1er
❶ 93 50 77 21 ❹ 12.00–15.00, 19.00–23.00 daily ⓝ Bus: 1, 2, 5, 6 to
Place Ste-Dévote

Vecchia Firenze £–££ ❾ A good place to head for lunch or dinner
if you happen to be near the station, where the choice otherwise
isn't great. Solid menu of pasta, pizza and other Mediterranean fare.
ⓐ 4 av Prince Pierre ❶ 93 30 27 70 ❹ 12.00–14.00, 19.00–22.30
Tues–Sun ⓝ Bus: 1, 2, 4, 5, 6 to Place d'Armes

Quai des Artistes ££ ❿ This chic Parisian-style bistro is one of the top
places for seafood and boasts a lively atmosphere. ⓐ 4 quai Antoine 1er
❶ 97 97 97 77 ⓦ www.quaidesartistes.com ❹ 12.30–14.30, 19.30–23.15
daily ⓝ Bus: 1, 2, 4, 5, 6 to Place d'Armes

BARS & CLUBS
As well as Stars'N'Bars (see opposite), lively late-night bars are:

La Rascasse This bar is located on the most famous corner of the
Monaco Grand Prix circuit. It features DJs and bands playing live, as
well as themed evenings. ⓐ Quai Antoine Premier ❹ 24.00–04.45
Mon–Fri, 24.00–05.00 Sat

Slammers A popular candle-lit hangout with two-for-one drinks
during happy hour (17.00–20.00). ⓐ 6 rue Suffren Reymond
❶ 97 70 36 56 ⓦ www.slammers-bar.com ❹ 17.00–01.00 daily
ⓝ Bus: 1, 2, 5, 6 to Stade Nautique

Fontvieille

Although Fontvieille is mainly residential, it contains a surprising number of museums, many of them clustered conveniently near the edge of the old town, as well as stadia, a sculpture trail and one of Monaco's most beautiful parks. The district is walkable and very accessible from other parts of Monaco. Bus routes 5 and 6 both connect Fontvieille with Place d'Armes, and Bus 5 travels to La Condamine while Bus 6 runs through Monte Carlo to Larvotto via the Casino.

SIGHTS & ATTRACTIONS

Helicopter trips

Fontvieille is the site of Monaco's heliport and, as well as operating the scheduled heli-taxi service to and from Nice's airport (see page 50), two helicopter companies offer a range of trips over the surrounding area, some of them combined with other pursuits such as golf, skiing and haute cuisine – even weddings. Typically a trip around Monaco will take 10–15 minutes; one taking in most of the Riviera 40–60 minutes. Fares start at €60 per person for a group of four passengers.

Héli Air Monaco ❷ Héliport de Monaco, Av des Ligures ❶ 92 05 00 50 ⓦ www.heliairmonaco.com ❷ Bus: 5, 6 to Héliport

Jardin Animalier (Zoo)

Close to the Terrasses de Fontvieille is Monaco's zoological garden, opened by the late Prince Rainier in 1954. Overlooking the Fontvieille harbour from the southern side of the Rocher de Monaco, this must be one of the most pleasantly situated zoos in the world. Although it's not large, it houses over 50 species of exotic birds and animals,

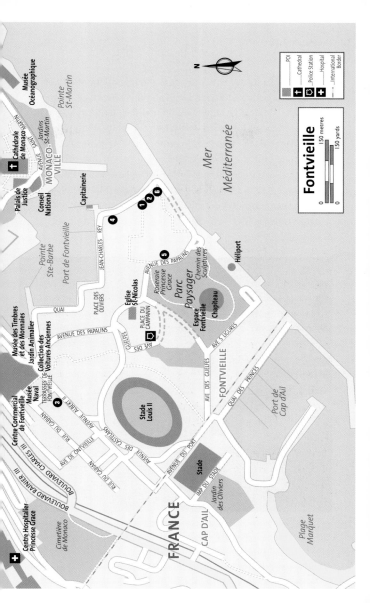

Musée
Océanographique

Pointe
St-Martin

Cathédrale
de Monaco

Palais de
Justice

Conseil
National

MONACO-
VILLE

Jardins
St-Martin

AVENUE SAINT

AVENUE SAINT-MARTIN

Capitainerie

Pointe
Ste-Barbe

Port de Fontvieille

JEAN-CHARLES REY

❹

❶❷❻

Mer
Méditerranée

Héliport

AVENUE DES PAPALINS

❺

Chemin des
Sculptures

Parc
Paysager

Roseraie
Princesse
Grace

Église
St-Nicolas

PLACE DES
OLIVIERS

Musée des Timbres
et des Monnaies

Jardin Animalier

Collection des
Voitures Anciennes

QUAI

AVENUE DES PAPALINS

PLACE DU
CAMPANIN

AVE DES
GUELFES

Espace
Fontvieille

Chapiteau

AVE DES GUELFES

FONTVIEILLE

AVE S LIGURES

QUAI DES PRINCES

Port de
Cap d'Ail

Centre Commercial
de Fontvieille

Musée
Naval

TERRASSES DE
FONTVIEILLE

❸

AVENUE ALBERT II

RUE DU GABIAN

AVE DE FONTVIEILLE

AVENUE DES CASTELANS

Stade
Louis II

RUE DU GABIAN

AVENUE DU PORT

Stade

IMP DU STADE

Jardin
des Oliviers

Centre Hospitalier
Princesse Grace

BOULEVARD RAINIER III

BOULEVARD CHARLES III

Cimetière
de Monaco

FRANCE

CAP D'AIL

Plage
Marquet

N

POI
Cathedral
Police Station
Hospital
International
Border

Fontvieille

0   150 metres
0   150 yards

including black panthers, white tigers and hippopotami, as well as lemurs, racoons and a wide range of reptiles. Because of space constraints, some of its larger inhabitants, including large primates and the former star resident, Margareth the white rhino, have had to be transferred to other zoos in recent years; nevertheless, this collection of birds and beasts is well cared-for and certain to appeal to younger visitors. ❸ 9 terrasses de Fontvieille or Espl Rainier III ❶ 93 50 40 30 ⏱ 10.00–12.00, 14.00–18.00 daily (Mar–May); 09.00–12.00, 14.00–19.00 daily (June–Sept); 10.00–12.00, 14.00–17.00 daily (Oct–Feb) ⊘ Bus: 1, 2, 4, 5, 6 to Place d'Armes. ❶ Admission charge

🔺 *The Chemin des Sculptures ends in the well-kept Parc Paysager de Fontvieille*

Parc Paysager de Fontvieille & Chemin des Sculptures

In the heart of Fontvieille, off Avenue des Papalins, lies this pleasant 4-hectare (10-acre) landscaped park, laid out with an impressive collection of trees and shrubs from all over the world and a small lake, populated by ducks and swans, in the middle. The nearby Chemin des Sculptures or 'Sculpture Trail' shows off a large number of the 100 or so modern sculptures that decorate the streets throughout Monaco (see page 46). In the middle of the park is the Espace Fontvieille, a large arena that is used to stage many shows and exhibitions, the most notable of which is the annual International Circus Festival in January. ⓐ Av des Papalins ⓦ www.montecarlofestival.mc ⓛ Dawn–dusk daily ⓝ Bus: 5, 6 to Roseraie

Roseraie Princesse Grace (Princess Grace Rose Garden)

Follow the sculpture trail and you will come to the Roseraie Princesse Grace, in the northeast corner of the Parc Paysager. The much-loved wife of Rainier III met her tragic death in a car accident in 1982; two years later, the Prince inaugurated this garden in her memory. Over 4,000 bushes, representing 150 varieties of rose, are planted here and their combined fragrance is overwhelming. ⓐ Next to Parc Paysager ⓛ Dawn–dusk daily ⓝ Bus: 5, 6 to Roseraie

Stade Louis II

This gigantic concrete stadium is no asset to Monaco visually, but it does provide the Principality with an Olympic-standard sports complex, including gymnasia, a running track and an indoor pool, and is the home ground of Monaco's high-flying football team, AS Monaco. It's possible to take a 45-minute guided tour with a commentary in English. ⓐ 3 av des Castelans ⓣ 92 05 40 11 ⓛ Tours at 09.30, 10.30,

11.00, 11.30, 14.30 and 16.00 Mon–Fri (mornings only on Wed)
🚍 Bus: 5, 6 to Stade Louis II ❶ Admission charge

Terrasses de Fontvieille

This terrace, overlooking the Port de Fontvieille (the smaller of
Monaco's two ports), is easily reached on foot from Place du Palais.
It is the home of Fontvieille's three museums (see opposite),
which are among Monaco's best, and the zoo. 🚍 Bus: 1, 2, 4, 5, 6
to Place d'Armes

🔻 *The Olympic-class Stade Louis II*

CULTURE

Three diverse collections occupy much of the Terrasses de Fontvieille, the closest part of the district to the old town.

Collection des Voitures Anciennes (Classic Car Exhibition)

This is the private collection of the late Prince Rainier III, who was an avid motorsports enthusiast and collector of cars that appealed to him, not just luxury or sports cars. From the 1903 De Dion Bouton to the legendary 1986 Lamborghini Countach, the perfectly maintained exhibits constitute a virtual history of 20th-century automobiles.
ⓐ Terrasses de Fontvieille ① 92 05 28 56 ① 10.00–18.00 daily
Ⓝ Bus: 1, 2, 4, 5, 6 to Place d'Armes ① Admission charge

Musée Naval (Maritime Museum)

Further along the Terrasses is this collection of scale models of famous ships, some 250 in all. Monaco has a long history of seafaring, from the Middle Ages (its small navy served the French kings against the English in the Hundred Years War) to the 20th century, when Prince Albert I sent scientific expeditions across the globe. Even if your interest in the subject is slight, you can't fail to be impressed by the detail and size of the models – for instance, that of the *Titanic* is over 3 m (10 ft) long; if you are into maritime history, or your kids are, you may find yourself spending several hours here. ⓐ 1 terrasses de Fontvieille ① 92 05 28 48 ⓦ www.musee-naval.mc ① 10.00–18.00 daily Ⓝ Bus: 1, 2, 4, 5, 6 to Place d'Armes ① Admission charge

Musée des Timbres et des Monnaies (Stamps & Coins Museum)

One of Monaco's traditional official sources of revenue, apart from the earnings of the casinos and associated hotels, has been in postage stamps. Long before most other countries realised the financial potential of philately, Monaco was regularly issuing collectible editions of stamps, distinguished by the quality of their artwork. The country began issuing its own coinage in 1640 and many of its coins are prized by collectors. This specialist museum commemorates the history of Monégasque stamps and coins with a well-presented exhibition displaying both the artefacts themselves and the changing technology used to make them. The Principality's historic output can be viewed in the new multimedia centre. Every paying visitor gets to take away a Monaco stamp. ❷ 11 terrasses de Fontvieille ❶ 98 98 41 50 ❶ 09.30–17.00 daily (Aug–June); 09.30–18.00 daily (July–Sept) ❷ Bus: 1, 2, 4, 5, 6 to Place d'Armes ❶ Admission charge

RETAIL THERAPY

The district's shopping is dominated by the huge Centre Commercial de Fontvieille, which sits squarely at the junction of Fontvieille and Monaco-Ville. Its large Carrefour hypermarket meets most of the needs of this residential district (and is very useful for virtually anything a visitor might need, from takeaway food to cheap clothing). There are many smaller specialist shops within the Centre, too. Add to that plenty of bars and cafés for R&R and you might find it a welcome contrast to the price tags (or lack of them) in the Monte Carlo boutiques.

TAKING A BREAK

The bars and cafés of Fontvieille cluster, naturally enough, on Quai Jean-Charles Rey, the southwest side of the Port de Fontvieille, from where you can look over the luxury yachts to the impressive flank of the Rocher du Monaco. The other good place for a quick lunchtime bite is the Centre Commercial de Fontvieille, which has several decent brasseries and pizzerias.

Gerhard's Café £ ❶ If only a good German-style beer will quench your thirst, you can't get better than the Fürstenberg at this quayside bar. ⓐ 42 quai Jean-Charles Rey ❶ 92 05 25 79 🕒 08.00–03.00 Mon–Sat, 18.00–03.00 Sun Ⓝ Bus: 5, 6 to Port de Fontvieille

Ship & Castle £ ❷ For those who prefer a pub atmosphere, this would-be piece of Old England is next door to Gerhard's. ⓐ 42 quai Jean-Charles Rey ❶ 92 05 76 72 🕒 11.00–01.00 Sun–Fri, 18.00–01.00 Sat Ⓝ Bus: 5, 6 to Port de Fontvieille

ZenZen £ ❸ ZenZen offers healthy Asian tapas in an upmarket fast food setting with an emphasis on ethics and fair trade. ⓐ 25 av Albert II ❶ 97 70 27 27 Ⓦ www.zenzen.com 🕒 09.00–22.00 Mon–Sat Ⓝ Bus: 5, 6 to Port de Fontvieille

AFTER DARK

RESTAURANTS
Cacio e Pepe £ ❹ Expect good food, friendly service and reasonable prices at this lovely Italian restaurant, as well as scrumptious home-made desserts. ⓐ 32 quai Jean-Charles Rey ❶ 97 70 33 11 🕒 12.00–15.00, 19.30–24.00 Mon–Sat Ⓝ Bus: 5, 6 to Port de Fontvieille

La Brasserie ££ ❺ This exceptional restaurant follows the same high standards as the hotel in which it is housed. ⓐ Hotel Columbus,

23 av des Papalins ☎ 92 05 90 00 🕐 12.00–14.00, 19.30–22.30 daily
🚌 Bus: 5, 6 to Port de Fontvieille

Beefbar ££–£££ ❻ Immensely popular Italian-run restaurant
specialising in high-quality cuts of meat and fish. Booking
is essential. 🏠 42 quai Jean-Charles Rey ☎ 97 77 09 29
🌐 www.beefbar.com 🕐 12.00–14.30, 20.00–23.30 daily 🚌 Bus: 5, 6
to Port de Fontvieille

ENTERTAINMENT

Espace Polyvalent Salle du Canton This entertainment venue near
the Centre Commercial has a varied programme of concerts, opera
and theatre, as well as discos and music festivals throughout the
year. It's worth checking the current programme with the tourist
office or via the website. 🏠 Terrasses de Fontvieille, 25–29 av Prince
Héréditaire Albert ☎ 93 10 12 10 🌐 www.salleducanton.mc 🕐 Box
office: 09.00–17.00 Mon–Fri 🚌 Bus: 1, 2, 4, 5, 6 to Place d'Armes

▶ *Menton occupies a prime position on the French Riviera*

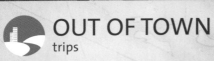

OUT OF TOWN

trips

Roquebrune-Cap-Martin & Menton

At one time, the Grimaldis of Monaco also ruled the neighbouring territories of Roquebrune-Cap-Martin and Menton to the northeast. By the mid-19th century both had been lost, albeit peacefully, to France. The proximity of these two French Riviera resorts makes them ideal destinations for a day (or even a half-day) out from Monaco. It would be possible to visit both in the same day, but to do them justice, allot a day to each. Roquebrune-Cap-Martin combines the picturesque attractions of an ancient hilltop village with the possibility of easy coastal walks round the Cap-Martin peninsula to the more modern resort area of Carnolès. Menton is a charming old port town that is as much Italian as French, and can claim to be the garden capital of the Riviera.

GETTING THERE

Both places are easily accessible by train from Monaco's railway station (see page 59): Roquebrune-Cap-Martin is only five minutes away, and Menton just a ten-minute journey. Trains are frequent – at least a dozen a day from early morning to mid-evening, and return trains leave Menton till as late as midnight. If you arrive at Roquebrune-Cap-Martin by rail, you'll have to climb a stepped path from the station up to the village, or take a taxi. Menton's railway station, however, is very central and a short, easy walk from the town centre and seafront.

If you're motoring, you can treat yourself to a drive along the winding Grande Corniche, or the slightly lower Moyenne Corniche, both of which have great views of the coast, for the passenger at least – the roads are famous for their hairpin corners. If you're not

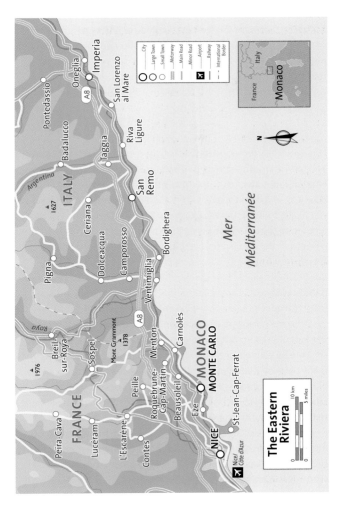

City

Large Town

Small Town

Main Road

Motorway

Minor Road

Railway

Airport

International Border

Monaco

Italy

France

Italy

Imperia

Oneglia

San Lorenzo al Mare

A8

Pontedassio

Badalucco

Riva Ligure

Taggia

Argentina

ITALY

▲ 1627

Ceriana

San Remo

Pigna

Dolceacqua

Camporosso

Bordighera

Ventimiglia

Mer Méditerranée

N

Roya

Breil-sur-Roya

Sospel

Mont Grammont 1378

Peille

MENTON

Carnolès

MONACO

MONTE CARLO

▲ 1976

Peïra-Cava

Lucéram

L'Escarène

Contes

FRANCE

Roquebrune-Cap-Martin

Beausoleil

Èze

St-Jean-Cap-Ferrat

NICE

Nice/ Côte d'Azur

The Eastern Riviera

10 km

5 miles

0

0

confident that you can take the corniches' bends, head out to the A8 *autoroute* and take exit 58 to Roquebrune-Cap-Martin, exit 59 for Menton. Roquebrune-Cap-Martin village is not suitable for motor traffic but there's plenty of parking outside it.

Roquebrune-Cap-Martin

This beautifully preserved fortified village overlooks the Mediterranean and the Cap-Martin peninsula. The maze of narrow streets was originally intended to confuse any enemy that penetrated the outer defences, as it does today's visitors – but it's too small to get seriously lost in. Just outside the village on the Chemin de Menton is what is reputed to be the world's oldest olive tree. The other main attraction, other than the atmosphere, is the Château de Roquebrune at the top of the village, with four floors of historical exhibits and a dungeon. Once a fortress of the princes of Monaco, it was designed to be garrisoned by no more than six men, and the tour gives a fascinating insight into medieval military and daily life.

From the railway station you can walk the coastal path around the foot of the Cap-Martin peninsula, and just round the bend of the Baie de Roquebrune you'll come across Le Cabanon. Among the many personalities who have chosen to live in this picturesque part of the world over the years was the architect Le Corbusier, and Le Cabanon was his beach shack; it is open to visitors by arrangement. Le Corbusier had strong views about the way the seaside was being developed, and Le Cabanon represents his solution – a kind of modular seaside cabin. Le Corbusier drowned while swimming in the bay in 1965, and his impressive, self-designed memorial can be seen in Roquebrune-Cap-Martin's cemetery.

🔺 *Picturesque Roquebrune-Cap-Martin is perched high above the eastern Riviera*

SIGHTS & ATTRACTIONS

Beaches You'll find two secluded beaches, Plage du Golfe Bleu and Plage du Buse, just below Roquebrune-Cap-Martin railway station.

Le Cabanon 🚩 Av Le Corbusier 🕐 Guided visits 09.30 Tues & Fri (ask at tourist office, see below) ❶ Admission charge

Château de Roquebrune 🚩 Pl William Ingram ❶ 00 33 4 93 35 07 22 🕐 10.00–12.30, 14.00–18.30 daily (Sept–June); 10.00–12.30, 15.00–19.30 daily (July & Aug) ❶ Admission charge

Tourist office This is actually in Carnolès, 2 km (1 mile) along the coast from Roquebrune-Cap-Martin village. 🚩 218 av Aristide Briand, Carnolès ❶ 00 33 4 93 35 62 87 🌐 www.roquebrune-cap-martin.com 🕐 09.00–12.30, 16.00–18.00 Mon–Sat

Walking The tourist office has a good map of recommended walks around Roquebrune-Cap-Martin and the Cap-Martin peninsula.

TAKING A BREAK

Roquebrune-Cap-Martin is not famed for its nightlife (it could hardly compete with Monte Carlo on its doorstep), but the area is well furnished with cafés and restaurants. Most of the pizzerias and budget eateries are in the built-up area of Carnolès, but you still have several options for a mid-morning or midday break in the old village itself: there are two restaurants for a leisurely lunch or atmospheric supper on Place des Deux Frères, a small square with great views across the bay to Monaco. Around the foot of

Cap-Martin you'll find several delightful seaside restaurants and cafés, as well as some lovely beaches.

Fraises et Chocolat £ A *salon de thé* in the old village that serves luscious gâteaux, as its name suggests: good for a mid-morning snack or light lunch. ➋ 1 rue Raymond Poincaré ➊ 00 33 6 67 08 32 20 Ⓦ www.lesdeuxfreres.com ➍ 08.00–18.00 Sat–Thur

La Grotte £ Grills and seafood are the specialities at this good-value café/restaurant in the village. ➋ Pl des Deux Frères ➊ 00 33 4 93 35 00 04 ➍ 12.00–14.15, 19.00–22.00 Thur evening– Tues (Dec–Oct)

Les Deux Frères ££ Gastronomic dining at this hotel restaurant, in the heart of the old village, is enhanced by the superb views from the terrace. ➋ Pl des Deux Frères ➊ 00 33 4 93 28 99 00 Ⓦ www.lesdeuxfreres.com ➍ 12.00–13.45, 19.30–21.30 Tues evening–Sun lunch; closed 15 Nov–15 Dec

Au Grand Inquisiteur ££ In the narrow winding streets of Roquebrune village, this restaurant has a medieval interior and old-style French cuisine. ➋ 15 rue Château ➊ 00 33 4 93 35 05 37 Ⓦ www.augrandinquisiteur.com ➍ 12.00–14.00, 19.00–21.30 Tues–Sun; closed in winter

L'Hippocampe ££–£££ A nice location for a leisurely lunch or early-evening meal on the far side of Cap-Martin, looking out over the sea from its dining terrace. Customers can also use its private beach. ➋ 44 av Winston Churchill ➊ 00 33 4 93 35 81 91 Ⓦ www.hippocampe-restaurant.com ➍ 12.00–14.30, 19.30–22.00 Tues–Sun; closed in winter

ACCOMMODATION

There are at least 11 hotels in this area, all of them close enough to the rail stations of Roquebrune-Cap-Martin and Carnolès to make commuting into Monaco a viable alternative to staying in the Principality.

Hôtel Alexandra £ In an attractive location on the east side of the Cap-Martin peninsula, with views across the bay of Menton towards Italy, the Alexandra has 40 rooms all with their own private bath, and is open all year round. ❸ 93 av Winston Churchill ❶ 00 33 4 93 35 65 45 Ⓦ www.hotel-alexandra.net

Le Roquebrune £ This *chambre d'hôte* (B&B) has six rooms, all with showers. A short walk from Roquebrune-Cap-Martin station, it's also convenient for the beaches and the village. ❸ 100 av Jean Jaures ❶ 00 33 4 93 35 00 16 Ⓦ www.le-roquebrune.com

Hôtel des Deux Frères £–££ The only hotel in the old village itself, this place is beautifully situated. ❸ Pl des Deux Frères ❶ 00 33 4 93 28 99 00 Ⓦ www.lesdeuxfreres.com

Menton

The town of Menton is only a stone's throw from Italy, as its architecture and pace of life confirm. Until it broke free in 1848, Menton belonged to the princes of Monaco, and it wasn't until 1860 that it voted to become part of France. The fact that it is also a prime retirement spot also adds to the quiet, contented atmosphere of the

⬤ *The architecture tells you that Menton was once part of Italy*

town. During the late 19th and early 20th centuries Menton was a magnet for British and Russian aristocrats wintering on the Riviera, but many of the belle époque hotels in which they stayed have now vanished or have been turned into apartments. Though no longer the most fashionable resort on the Riviera, Menton still has a refined air, but is certainly not stuffy. For a long time popular with well-to-do French and Italian holidaymakers, it now sees a growing number of visitors from overseas.

Its superb microclimate is what draws the retirees and makes Menton the lemon-growing capital of France, as well as guaranteeing the health of the exotic shrubs that decorate its public and private gardens so attractively. On Shrove Tuesday you can have all the lemons you want with your pancakes – it's the day the town celebrates its principal crop with the exuberant Lemon Festival. If you're seriously interested in citrus fruits, then you should also make a beeline for La Citronneraie, a fragrant orchard that is Europe's leading collection of the plants of this species (the orchard is privately owned – access details from the tourist office).

The artist, writer and film director Jean Cocteau spent the last years of his life in Menton. Lasting memorials to him include the Salle des Mariages (wedding hall) of the town hall, which he decorated with vast, surreal frescoes, and the Musée Jean Cocteau, in a medieval bastion on the waterfront – the exhibits illustrate the versatility of his talents. Other notables who have lived and died in Menton, and are buried in the Cimetière du Vieux-Château high up in the town, include the British artist Aubrey Beardsley and William Webb Ellis, the inventor of rugby.

The modern centre of Menton is dominated by the twin avenues Verdun and Boyer, which are separated by the Jardins Biovès. At their southern end is the Casino Barrière de Menton, which sits on

◆ Menton's Lemon Festival is a popular annual event

the main seafront parade, the Promenade du Soleil. Some of the best views of Menton are from the Vieux Port, the old harbour just east of the town centre. This area also offers a wide choice of cafés and bistros. The district behind the Vieux Port is the oldest part of town, the pedestrianised area known as Vieux Menton. Here you will find picture-postcard-pretty Italianate buildings huddled around the Basilica of St Michel and the Chapelle des Pénitents Blancs (the chapel of the medieval brotherhood of white-robed penitents).

Gardening enthusiasts will be pleased to hear that Menton is a premier *Ville Fleurie* of France and boasts the motto 'My City is a Garden'. Exotic gardens in or near the town include the Spanish-style Fontana Rosa, Le Val Rahmeh (tropical and subtropical plants, especially Solanaceae) and La Serre de la Madone (planted in the 1920s by Lawrence Johnston, creator of Britain's Hidcote Garden). The Giardini Botanici Hanbury (see page 130) are also accessible from the town. A full list of parks and gardens, all worth a visit, is obtainable at the tourist office.

There's usually an event taking place on the streets of Menton, whenever you choose to visit. Apart from the 15-day Lemon Festival in February, the town hosts music festivals in May, July (including a Tango Festival, when the town takes on a South American theme) and August (with dancing in the streets during the 'Animations d'Eté'). In June private gardens are opened to the public. Children of all ages may prefer the Menton Grand Prix in August – it's for go-karts.

SIGHTS & ATTRACTIONS

Beaches After (or instead of) all that strenuous garden visiting, you may fancy a spot of swimming or sunbathing. Menton has well-kept, sandy beaches and the water quality has earned it an EU Blue Flag. Most of the beaches are private, attached to a café or restaurant, and charge an entrance fee, but the Plage des Sablettes is public and free.

Centre Internationale de Plongée de la Maïna Menton's centre for diving and similar underwater activities. ⓐ 3 prom de la Mer ⓣ 00 33 4 93 35 95 83 Ⓦ www.palmesbeach.fr ⓛ 09.00–19.00 daily

Centre Nautique If you are interested in any of Menton's wide offering of watersports, this branch of the tourist office should be your first port of call for information on everything from surfboarding to kayaking. ⓐ 8 prom de la Mer ⓣ 00 33 4 93 35 49 70 Ⓦ www.voile-menton.fr ⓛ 08.30–19.00 daily (Apr–Aug); 08.30–18.00 daily (Sept–Mar)

Fontana Rosa ⓐ Pl Blasco Ibanez, about 2 km (1¼ miles) east of town ⓣ 00 33 4 92 41 76 76 ⓛ Guided visits 10.00 Fri ⓦ Bus: 3 to Blasco Ibanez ⓘ Admission charge

Koaland Children's and family entertainment and activities, with mini-golf, go-karts, rides including a mini-roller coaster, bouncy castles and other diversions, about 1 km (²⁄₃ mile) outside the town. ⓐ 5 av de la Madone ⓣ 00 33 4 92 10 00 40 ⓛ 10.00–12.00, 14.00–18.00 Wed–Mon (Sept–June); 10.00–12.00, 16.00–24.00 Wed–Mon (July & Aug)

Musée Jean Cocteau ⓐ Bastion du Vieux Port ⓣ 00 33 4 93 57 72 30 ⓛ 10.00–12.30, 14.00–18.00 Wed–Mon ⓘ Admission charge

Salle des Mariages ⓐ Mairie (Town Hall), Pl Ardoïno ⓣ 00 33 4 92 10 50 00 ⓛ 08.30–12.30, 14.00–16.30 Mon–Fri (except public holidays) ⓘ Admission charge

La Serre de la Madone ⓐ 74 route de Gorbio, about 3 km (2 miles) northwest of Menton town centre ⓣ 00 33 4 93 57 73 90 ⓦ www.serredelamadone.com ⓛ 10.00–18.00 Tues–Sun (Apr–Sept); guided visits 15.00 Tues–Sun (Apr–Sept) ⓝ Bus: 7 to Val de Gorbio ⓘ Admission charge

Tourist office ⓐ Palais de l'Europe, 8 av Boyer ⓣ 00 33 4 92 41 76 76 ⓦ www.tourisme-menton.fr ⓛ 08.30–12.30, 14.00–19.00 Mon–Sat, 14.00–18.00 Sun

Le Val Rahmeh ⓐ Av St-Jacques ⓣ 00 33 4 93 35 86 72 ⓛ 10.00–12.30, 15.30–18.30 daily (Apr–Sept); 14.00–17.00 daily (Oct–Mar) ⓝ Bus: 3 to Stade ⓘ Admission charge

RETAIL THERAPY

Menton attracts the sort of residents and visitors who can afford luxury goods, and shops catering to their tastes congregate on Avenue Félix Faure and Avenue de Verdun in the middle of town. For smaller specialist boutiques shops, head for Vieux Menton.

Markets Produce markets take place every morning in the covered market hall (ⓐ Quai de Monléons) and at the Marché du Careï (ⓐ Prom Maréchal Leclerc), and there are *brocante* (bric-a-brac) markets on Fridays (ⓐ Espl Palmero) and on the second Sunday of each month (ⓐ Espl du Bastion).

Prestige de Menton Beauty products, perfumes, Bach flower remedies, essential oils and the local speciality *Eau de Menton* are on sale here. ⓐ 19 rue Saint Michel ⓣ 00 33 4 93 47 45 87

TAKING A BREAK

Basilico £ An affordable and friendly establishment with swift service and excellent Italian cuisine. ⓐ 1 sq Victoria ⓣ 00 33 4 93 35 76 04 ⓛ 12.00–14.00, 19.30–22.30 daily

Le Petit Port £ A cosy restaurant offering a wide range of traditional home-made French and Provençal dishes. ⓐ 4 rue Jonquier ⓣ 33 4 93 35 82 62 ⓛ 12.00–14.30, 19.30–22.00 daily

Al Vicoletto £–££ One of the best Italian restaurants on the Côte d'Azur, where chef Guido Forastieri prepares pizzas, pasta, cakes and other specialities from Calabria. ⓐ 40 rue Patourneaux, Impasse Bellecour (next to Pl St Roch) ⓣ 00 33 4 93 28 18 40 ⓛ 12.00–14.30, 19.30–22.00 daily

Au Pistou £–££ Good seafood and local Mentonnais cuisine is offered at this harbourside restaurant. ⓐ Quai Gordon Bennett ⓣ 00 33 4 93 57 45 89 ⓛ Times vary

Le Galet £–££ The restaurant of the Hôtel Princesse & Richmond, facing the sea, serves classic Mediterranean cuisine. ⓐ 617 prom du Soleil ⓣ 00 33 4 93 35 80 20 ⓦ www.princessrichmond.com ⓛ 19.00–22.00 Mon & Wed, 12.00–14.30, 19.00–22.00 Thur–Sun

AFTER DARK

Casino Barrière de Menton More low-key than the casinos in Monte Carlo, this establishment offers roulette (French and English), blackjack and 150 slot machines. There's also a disco on Saturday

Flowery Menton revels in year-round sunshine

evenings. 📍 Av Félix Faure ☎ 00 33 4 92 10 16 16 🌐 www.lucien
barriere.com 🕐 10.00–03.00 (slots); 20.00–03.00 Sun–Thur,
19.00–04.00 Fri & Sat (gaming tables)

ACCOMMODATION

There's plenty of accommodation in and around the town. For an
overview, visit 🌐 www.hotelmenton.com

Auberge de Jeunesse £ Menton's youth hostel makes up for the lack
of hostel facilities in Monaco itself. It's just above town, only a short
walk from the centre. 📍 Plateau de St-Michel ☎ 00 33 4 93 35 93 14
🌐 www.hihostels.com

Hôtel Chambord £ Just a short walk from the seafront, this
welcoming and distinctive hotel is close to the city centre and
far from the noise of the busy beach promenade. Rooms are bright
and modern with free Wi-Fi. 📍 6 av Boyer ☎ 00 33 4 93 35 94 19
🌐 www.hotel-chambord.com

L'Aiglon £–££ A handsome white villa of the belle époque houses one
of the best hotels on this part of the Riviera. The décor is traditional
and it has a garden and pool. By the Parc de la Madone, about 1 km
(⅔ mile) from the centre. 📍 7 av de la Madone ☎ 00 33 4 93 57 55 55
🌐 www.hotelaiglon.net

Hôtel Napoléon £–££ Right on the Menton seafront, this hotel
has rooms with sea views and balconies, plus a private beach
and outdoor pool. 📍 29 porte de France ☎ 00 33 4 93 35 89 50
🌐 www.napoleon-menton.com

Ventimiglia & San Remo

As well as being a great base for visiting the French Riviera, Monaco is also a gateway to the other Riviera – the Ligurian one, just over the border in Italy. The resorts along this stretch of coastline are not as famous as their French counterparts, but the two most popular day-trip destinations, Ventimiglia and San Remo, are well worth a visit. Ventimiglia (usually spelt 'Vintimille' on French maps) is only just over the Franco-Italian border, and San Remo, the biggest resort on the Ligurian Riviera, is just 35 km (22 miles) from Monaco.

GETTING THERE

The easiest way to reach either town is by train from Monaco's railway station (see page 59). There are at least a dozen trains on weekdays and Saturdays, and only slightly fewer on Sundays, running from around 06.00 until the early evening. Check the timetables carefully at the station before deciding on your itinerary, and take note that there are a handful of express trains that require seat reservation in advance. The last regular train back to Monaco from Ventimiglia is at around 23.00, although there are also a few night trains. Ventimiglia is a 24-minute journey and San Remo is just over an hour away.

If you're driving, simply join the A8 motorway just outside Monaco and follow the signs east for Menton and Italy. The border crossing is just past Menton and there are no formalities (but there may be customs checks in the opposite direction – see page 131); the motorway becomes the A10 in the Italian numbering system. Exits are well signposted. The journey times to both towns are similar to those of the trains, taking into account how long it takes to get from Monaco to the motorway and from the motorway to the town centres. There is also a winding coastal road that connects Monaco with both places via Menton, which will take you past the Giardini Botanici Hanbury (see page 130) – the views from it are great, but it will take you considerably longer.

Ventimiglia

In the days before open frontiers in the EU, Ventimiglia's economy depended to a large extent on its position close to the border and the potential for duty-free shopping. Having lost that role to a great extent (though it still has a weekly market that lures French and foreign visitors across the border), it still has a long way to go in developing the tourism potential of its position, climate and antiquity.

FLOWER POWER
The coastline from the French border to San Remo has been dubbed the Riviera dei Fiori (Coast of Flowers) by the Italians, and not without reason. Not only is it graced by some outstanding public gardens, such as the Giardini Botanici Hanbury at La Mortola (see page 130), but the climate makes this a prime spot for growing flowers as a crop. The canny Ligurians switched from lemon growing to floriculture in the early 1900s and today export blooms all over Europe. Devotees of the Viennese New Year's Day Concert, which is broadcast all over the world, will know that the stupendous floral arrangements that always decorate the concert hall are an annual gift from (and a superb advertisement for) the flower-growers of San Remo.

The town was old even before the Romans colonised it, calling it Albintimilium (from which comes its modern name, even though this sounds like the Italian for 'twenty miles', and is even spelt 'XX miglia' on some maps). At the nearby Balzi Rossi (Red Rocks) Prehistoric Museum you can still see the caves that were inhabited by Homo erectus, a predecessor of Homo sapiens.

The old walled medieval town, Ventimiglia Alta, sits on a steep hill apart from the modern centre. Its twisty streets and alleys are more medieval in atmosphere than those of Monaco-Ville or other Riviera towns, and there are great mountain and sea views from the old walls. The old town has two particularly interesting churches. The Cathedral of the Assumption has a crypt dating from the seventh century that is probably part of an old Roman temple of the goddess Juno. The Church of San Michele will attract devotees of *The Da Vinci Code*, as it has documented Templar connections and is one of the reputed hiding places of the Holy Grail – which may explain why it's always locked.

New Ventimiglia is mainly a day-trip shopping destination (see page 130). If you arrive in July or August you'll be able to enjoy the Battle of the Flowers (July) or the costumed parades of the Medieval August Festival. The old town has a summer-long festival of pasta with street parties, the Sagra del Raviolo.

Tourist office IAT Ventimiglia ❸ Via Hambury 2, Ventimiglia
❶ 00 39 0184 35 11 83 Ⓦ www.visitrivieradeifiori.it

SIGHTS & ATTRACTIONS

Balzi Rossi Prehistoric Museum ❸ Via Balzi Rossi 9 ❶ 00 39 0184 38 113 ❶ 0900–12.30, 14.00–18.00 Tues–Sun (summer); 09.00–13.00, 16.30–18.00 Tues–Sun (winter)

● Ventimiglia is less geared to tourism than its neighbours, which adds to its charm

Giardini Botanici Hanbury (Gardens of the Villa Hanbury)

Just outside Ventimiglia, on the small promontory of La Mortola, is one of the world's most visited botanic gardens. English botanist Sir Thomas Hanbury, who had made a fortune as a trader in Shanghai, bought the site in 1867 and devoted the rest of his life to laying it out, with the intention of creating an unparalleled collection of plants from all over the world that could thrive in the mild climate here. The care of the garden was taken over after World War I by his daughter-in-law Lady Dorothy Hanbury, and between the two world wars La Mortola was so famous that *The Times* of London would print a list of all the plants in flower there in their New Year's Day edition. Sadly, during World War II the garden found itself in a battle zone and ended up in ruins. It was sold to the Italian state in 1960 and after a long period of inadequate funding was given to the care of the University of Genoa, which, thanks in great part to the agitation of British garden enthusiasts, is now restoring it to its former glory.

Of its 18 hectares (44 acres), half are given over to native Ligurian plants and half to exotic specimens. Enthusiasts can follow a long path down to the coast and marvel at the range of plants that will grow here. Highlights include an Australian forest, a Japanese garden and a collection of Far Eastern cycads. ➌ Corso Montecarlo 43, Cap Mortola, Ventimiglia ➊ 00 39 0184 22 95 07 ➍ www.amicihanbury. com ➋ 09.30–18.00 (1 Mar–15 June & 16 Sept–15 Oct); 09.30–19.00 (16 June–15 Sept); 09.30–17.00 (16 Oct–28 Feb); last admission one hour before closing ➍ Bus: 1 to La Mortola ➊ Admission charge

RETAIL THERAPY

Apart from the lure of the 'designer' bargains in Ventimiglia market, the main shopping attractions of the Ligurian Riviera are culinary.

The region is famed for its gourmet food and drink, and high-quality olive oil, pesto, pasta and the local wines are all worth hunting out in the markets and shops of the two towns.

Ventimiglia new town still sticks to its pre-border shopping ethos; it has the highest concentration of off-licences in Italy, and although there's now no duty-free logic to purchasing there, competition and the high volume of traffic keep prices low. However, the main shopping draw is the Friday market on the seafront of the new town, which extends around the public gardens and along Via Lungo, attracting French residents and tourists with its cheap olive oil and other foodstuffs, and the wide range of 'designer' goods on sale. How do you know they're fakes? Just look at the prices.

BUYER BEWARE

Whatever your own views on the ethics of trading in goods that are imitations of the authentic branded items, you should be aware that buying as well as selling them is illegal in the EU. The Italian authorities have done little to control the trade in Ventimiglia market, apart from a very small number of high-profile arrests of traders (and some shoppers) for the benefit of the media. On the other hand, the French police and customs, with no vested interest in the continuation of the market, have been taking a tough line, stopping tourist cars at the border, confiscating contraband 'designer' merchandise and destroying it in front of the tearful purchasers (and the TV cameras). Before you hand over your cash for that bargain item, bear in mind that it may not make it past the border.

To see everything the market has to offer, you'll need to get there early on Friday morning (the market starts at about 08.00 and goes on till 17.00 Nov–Apr and 18.00 May–Oct) and remember to haggle like mad. If you pay more than 50 per cent of the initial asking price you've been duped. Be aware also that the trains to Ventimiglia are very crowded on Fridays, for obvious reasons, and that if you're driving there you may have to park some way out of town.

TAKING A BREAK & AFTER DARK

Liguria is the original home of pesto and focaccia, and is proud of its distinctive cuisine. It would be a pity not to sample some of it while in Ventimiglia or San Remo. Less well known specialities include the local fishermen's pizza, known as *sardenaira*, which incorporates anchovies, vegetables and tomato but no cheese. The region's wines are hard to obtain elsewhere and a bottle or two would make a great souvenir – look out for the light, fresh red Rossese di Dolceacqua and the fragrant white Vermentino.

Although there is no nightlife to speak of in this area, Ventimiglia has a number of seafront cafés in which you can relax after buying your bargains at the Friday market. To experience some of the excellent pasta for which Liguria is famed, try any of the following establishments:

Sale e Pepe £ Great fish and seafood dishes, as well as pizzas and pastas. Popular with locals. ⓐ Passeggiata Oberdan 45 ⓣ 00 39 0184 23 07 14 ⓦ www.salepeperistorante.eu ⓛ 19.30–22.00 Tues–Thur, 12.00–14.00, 19.30–20.00 Fri–Sun

Marco Polo £–££ Lovely old restaurant right on the seafront, with an original take on Mediterranean cuisine. ⓐ Passeggiata Cavallotti 2

🕿 00 39 0184 35 26 78 🕐 19.30–22.00 Tues–Thur, 12.00–14.00, 19.30–22.00 Fri–Sun

Pasta e Basta £–££ Popular with French visitors, this hotel restaurant serves imaginative pasta dishes in large portions. Booking advisable.
🅐 Passeggiata Marconi 20, Marina San Giuseppe 🕿 00 39 0184 23 08 78
🕐 Lunch Fri–Sun, dinner Tues–Sun (times vary)

San Remo

The old name of San Remo was Matuzia, supposedly a reference to Matuta, the Roman goddess of the dawn. The town lies in an inlet between Capo Verde and Capo Nero, and is blessed with perhaps the best climate of any Riviera resort, French or Italian, hence its importance as a flower-growing centre. It's a lively seaside resort that hosts some important festivals and has an old quarter well worth a visit. At one time it was an important commercial port under the rule of the city-state of Genoa, but the old harbour (now the Porto Vecchio) silted up and the modern port (Portosole) shelters a fishing fleet, as well as the usual cluster of luxury yachts. San Remo's seafaring tradition is embodied today in the Porto Vecchio area, which offers a pleasant half-hour stroll from Piazza Bresca along the Corso delle Nazioni as far as the 18th-century fort of Santa Tecla, which once housed the garrison of the town's Genoese rulers before becoming a prison, and now awaits redevelopment as a tourist attraction.

Pigna, the walled medieval quarter, dates back over 1,000 years and its medieval streets wind their way up the hillside to the Church of the Sanctuary of Madonna della Costa and the Cathedral of San

Siro, dating from the 12th century and later rebuilt in Baroque style. Just outside the old town, in Piazza Eroi Sanremesi, stands the Torre della Ciapela with its 1-m (3-ft) stone walls, once part of the town's fortifications.

Modern San Remo was discovered by the same mix of British, Russian and other European plutocrats who put Monaco and Nice on the map, and consequently exhibits some fine architecture of the late 19th century, particularly of the exuberant style known to the Italians as 'Liberty' and to the French and Anglo-Saxons as 'Art Nouveau'. Like all self-respecting Riviera resorts it has a turn-of-the-century casino, built in 1905 and very fashionable in its day: past patrons included King Faroukh of Egypt and the Italian cinema star Vittorio de Sica, who claimed to have lost enough money there to have paid for its construction.

Fans of belle époque architecture can stroll the Corso degli Inglesi and view some beautiful examples of Art Nouveau and other styles in the villas that line it (nearly all privately owned and not open to the public). Of particular interest is the Villa Nobel, built in a so-called 'Moorish' style by the eponymous Swedish scientist and arms magnate, on Corso Cavalotti in eastern San Remo. It was while living here in the 1890s that Nobel decided to establish the prizes that bear his name; today it houses a Nobel museum.

This and many of the other villas possess splendid gardens that show off the range of exotic plants that will grow happily in San Remo, and many of the gardens are open to walk round. Clearly not wishing to be outdone by neighbouring Menton for the 'city of flowers' title, the municipality also provides magnificent floral displays in the public gardens, parks and flowerbeds all over town.

Further evidence of the heyday of San Remo's history as a resort for wealthy foreigners can be seen in the luxury Art Nouveau hotels,

San Remo specialises in year-round floral displays

over 20 of which have since been turned to other uses (the town hall was once the Hotel Bellevue), as well as the Russian Orthodox church, built on the orders of Tsarina Maria Alexandrovna in 1913.

San Remo's civic museum is housed in the 15th-century Palazzo Borea d'Olmo in Via Matteotti: the collection is mainly of archaeological and prehistoric finds but also includes a section devoted to mementos of Garibaldi, one of the founders of modern Italy. The other major cultural centre is the Rambaldi Art Gallery, with a worthy collection of Italian and Flemish masters.

Throughout the year the town hosts a full programme of events, the most important of which is the Italian Song Festival in February at the Teatro Ariston. This competition attracts not only the best of new Italian singers but also internationally known foreign artists. In March San Remo consolidates its position as Italy's flower capital with the festival **Sanremo in Fiore** (Ⓦ www. sanremoinfiore.it).

Sports enthusiasts may be more interested in the San Remo Rally, a World Championship car rally in October, and the succession of internationally attended sailing regattas that take place in November and December. The town also puts on a show-jumping competition over several weekends from April to October. For information see Ⓦ www.sanremomanifestazioni.it

SIGHTS & ATTRACTIONS

Civic Museum ⓐ Corso Matteotti 143 ❶ 00 39 0184 53 19 42
🕓 09.00–12.00, 15.00–18.00 Tues–Sat

Rambaldi Gallery ⓐ Piazza San Sebastiano 17 ❶ 00 39 0184 67 03 98
🕓 09.00–13.00, 14.30–17.30 Sat & Sun

🔺 *The Russian Orthodox church in San Remo*

Tourist office APT Riviera dei Fiori in San Remo covers the entire coast.
ⓐ Largo Nuvoloni 1 ❶ 00 39 0184 59 059 ⓦ www.rivieradeifiori.it

Villa Nobel ⓐ Corso Cavallotti 116 ❶ 00 39 0184 50 73 80
ⓦ www.villanobel.provincia.imperia.it ❷ 10.00–12.00 Tues–Thur;
10.00–12.00, 15.00–18.00 Fri & Sat

RETAIL THERAPY

San Remo's market is held on Tuesdays and Saturdays in the Piazza
Eroi Sanremesi near the old Pigna quarter; the atmosphere is less
touristy and more local than at Ventimiglia's.

TAKING A BREAK

There's a wide choice of pizzerias and restaurants in San Remo
and you'll never be far from a café in Pigna, on the seafront or
around the Porto Vecchio/Piazza Bresca area.

Graziella £ This is Italy, so you've got the perfect excuse to dig
your teeth into a tasty pizza. A good place to find one is this large
and friendly pizzeria in the market square outside the Pigna area.
ⓐ Piazza Eroi Sanremesi 48 ❶ 00 39 0184 50 22 50 ❷ 12.00–14.30,
19.30–22.00 daily

Pravda Café £ Enjoy Italian cuisine in this classic café in the
heart of old San Remo, which is also a great place for cocktails.
On Fridays Russian cuisine is served with music to accompany it.
ⓐ Piazza San Siro 16 ❶ 00 39 0184 59 18 29 ❷ Lunch and dinner
Mon–Sat (times vary)

▲ San Remo's Porto Vecchio is a good place to take a break

Urbicia Vivas £–££ Family-run restaurant with very helpful and friendly owners and an excellent choice of local cuisine. ❸ Piazza dei Dolori 5 ❶ 00 39 0184 57 55 66 ❿ www.urbiciavivas.com ❺ 12.00–14.00, 20.00–22.30 Tues–Sat

Biribissi ££–£££ If you haven't already lost all your cash in the San Remo Casino (see below), enjoy high-class international cuisine in its highly regarded restaurant. ❸ San Remo Casino, Corso degli Inglesi 18 ❶ 00 39 0184 52 83 ❺ Evenings only from 18.00 but times vary so call to book

AFTER DARK

San Remo Casino This is the main focus of nightlife in San Remo. In addition to gambling – mainly roulette, *chemin de fer* and slot machines – it has a lovely roof garden and incorporates an opera house, both of which stage a full programme of entertainment, and there's an excellent restaurant on-site, too. Check the Casino website or with the tourist office for the current programme of events. ❸ Corso degli Inglesi 18 ❶ 00 39 0184 59 51 ❿ www.casinosanremo.it ❺ 14.30–early morning ❶ Admission charge and jacket-and-tie dress code

▶ *Monaco's modern railway station*

PRACTICAL
information

Directory

GETTING THERE
By air
Nice Côte d'Azur Airport serves flights from many UK and Irish airlines, including Aer Lingus (from Dublin and Cork), British Airways, British Midland and bmibaby (from Birmingham and East Midlands), and easyJet (from London Gatwick, Luton and Stansted, Bristol, Liverpool, Newcastle and Belfast). Flight time from London is about two hours. Direct flights from other countries include Canada (Air Transat from Montreal, flight time 7 hrs 25 mins) and the USA (Air France, Delta from New York JFK, flight time 8 hrs 40 mins).

Many people are aware that air travel emits CO_2, which contributes to climate change. You may be interested in the possibility of lessening the environmental impact of your flight through the charity **Climate Care** (Ⓦ www.jpmorganclimatecare.com), which offsets your CO_2 by funding environmental projects around the world.

By rail
From London St Pancras International by Eurostar to Paris (Gare du Nord) and then by TGV direct to Monaco can be cheaper than an airline ticket. There are several TGV trains per day from Paris (Gare de Lyon) to Nice – more in summer. A few of them continue on to Monaco-Monte Carlo; the others have connections at Nice. The through train takes just over six hours, slightly more if you have to change at Nice. You can avoid Paris by changing from Eurostar at Lille Europe for the train to Nice and Monaco, which departs from Lille at 10.30 and gets to Nice at 18.04 – see timetables at www.voyages-sncf.com. The monthly *Thomas Cook European Rail Timetable* has up-to-date schedules for European international and national train services.

Eurostar reservations (UK) ☎ 08432 186 186 Ⓦ www.eurostar.com
Thomas Cook European Rail Timetable ☎ (UK) 01733 416477;
(USA) 1 800 322 3834 Ⓦ www.thomascookpublishing.com

By road
Driving from the UK via Calais will take two to three days to cover the
1,200 km (720 miles) from Calais to Monaco: head for Aix-en-Provence
and pick up the A8 motorway 'La Provencale', exiting at junction 56 for
Monaco. For a more scenic approach, you can leave the motorway at
Nice and follow one of the corniche mountain roads into Monaco.

ENTRY FORMALITIES
Monaco applies the same immigration and customs regulations as
France. Since entry to Monaco is from France, there are no formalities
at the Monégasque border. You should, however, be prepared for
a random stop and search by police.

Passports are needed by all foreign visitors, except EU citizens
who can produce a national identity card. Citizens of the UK and
other EU countries, and of the USA, Canada, Australia and New
Zealand, do not require a visa for visits of up to three months.
Other travellers should consult the French embassy or tourist

TRAVEL INSURANCE
Monaco is not a member of the EU, and UK visitors cannot
take advantage of reciprocal health insurance. Healthcare
facilities in the Principality are excellent but expensive; all
visitors to Monaco should, therefore, carry travel insurance
which provides generous medical cover.

office in their own country about visa requirements, or check on the official government website **France Diplomatie** ⓦ www.diplomatie.gouv.fr

Residents of the UK, Ireland and other EU countries may bring personal possessions and goods for personal use into France, including a reasonable amount of tobacco and alcohol, provided they have been bought in the EU. There are few formalities at the point of entry into France. Residents of non-EU countries, and EU residents arriving from a non-EU country, may bring in up to 200 cigarettes or 50 cigars or 250 g (8 oz) tobacco; 2 litres (two to three bottles) of wine and 1 litre (one bottle) of spirits or liqueurs. The full regulations and definitions of 'reasonable amount' may be checked at ⓦ www.douane.gouv.fr

MONEY

The euro (€) is the official currency of Monaco, even though it is not an EU member, so there's no need to change currency when entering from France. €1 = 100 cents. It comes in notes of €5, €10, €20, €50, €100, €200 and €500. Coins are in denominations of €1 and €2, and 1, 2, 5, 10, 20 and 50 cents.

ATM machines that accept British and international debit and credit cards are not plentiful. Those at the following locations are all open 24 hours daily:

Centre Commercial de Fontvieille ❷ 23 av Prince Héréditaire Albert (the main shopping centre in Fontvieille)

Crédit Foncier de Monaco ❸ 11 blvd Albert 1er (facing the harbour)

Crédit Mutuel ❷ 8 rue Grimaldi (La Condamine, near the market and shopping area)

The most widely accepted credit cards are Visa and MasterCard, though other major credit cards such as American Express are also accepted in restaurants and shops. Traveller's cheques and foreign money can be cashed at most banks and bureaux de change – you will have to produce your passport or other ID. Traveller's cheques are not widely accepted by restaurants and shops. Many hotels also change currency and cash traveller's cheques, though not always at a very favourable rate.

HEALTH, SAFETY & CRIME

Tap water is safe to drink (if not, it is marked *eau non potable*) but the locals and most visitors prefer to consume one of the many brands of mineral water. Medical facilities in Monaco are of an excellent standard, but expensive – ensure you have adequate travel insurance. Most minor ailments can be taken to pharmacies, indicated by a green cross sign. Pharmacies have expert staff who are qualified to offer medical advice and dispense a wide range of

● *Don't worry, the police are never far away in Monaco*

medicines. Many drugs, such as aspirin, that are widely available in the UK are obtainable only at pharmacies in Monaco.

Monaco has one of the highest police-to-population ratios in the world, as well as video surveillance on nearly every street, and you would be very unlucky to be the victim of a crime of any kind. Although it is only common sense to keep money and valuables out of sight, both on your person and if left in a car, this is one place where you could comfortably wear your best jewellery in public (and, of course, given the average wealth of the residents, they often do). If you do encounter any trouble or lose any property, you won't have any problem locating one of the *gendarmes* on the street, or you can report it at the central police station, which is in La Condamine, one block away from the harbour.

Police ❶ 17 or 112

Sureté Publique ❸ 3 rue Louis Notari ❶ 93 15 30 15
ⓦ www.police.gouv.mc ⓛ 24 hrs daily

OPENING HOURS

Banks ⓛ 09.00–12.00, 14.00–16.00 Mon–Fri; closed on national holidays.

Shops ⓛ 09.00–12.00, 14.00–19.00 Mon–Sat

TOILETS

The standard of public toilets (marked by a *Toilettes* sign) is high and they can be found all over the Principality. In addition, museums, shopping centres, cafés and restaurants all have good facilities.

CHILDREN

Although Monaco is usually thought of as a playground for adults rather than children, there's plenty here to make a family holiday a

The Nouveau Musée National de Monaco is a worthwhile trip with kids

success, especially as so many Riviera beaches are only a short drive away. Certainly, older children will enjoy many of Monaco's attractions – the model ships in the Musée Naval (see page 105), the shark tank in the Musée Océanographique (see page 84), the Collection des Voitures Anciennes (see page 105), the stalactites in the Grotte de l'Observatoire (see page 92), and the dolls in the Nouveau Musée National de Monaco (see page 66) all have potential child appeal. The little red-and-white tourist train is also a treat for children (see page 58). Its circuit takes you from Place d'Armes to Port Hercule, taking in the Formula 1 Grand Prix track, Monte Carlo and the old town. And if you really want to give them a treat, you can fork out for a helicopter trip around Monaco (see page 100). For younger kiddies the Parc Princesse Antoinette (see page 93) offers a supervised playground and a mini-golf course, and you can safely leave your young ones to be entertained by the qualified team at one of the children's clubs at the Plage du Larvotto while you finish off your tan (see page 67).

COMMUNICATIONS
Internet
Most top hotels now have Wi-Fi connections for guests. There is also an Internet café at this centrally located bar/restaurant:
Stars'N'Bars (see page 98) ⓐ 6 quai Antoine 1er ❶ 97 97 95 95
ⓦ www.starsnbars.com ❶ 11.00–24.00 Mon–Thur, 11.00–02.00 Fri–Sun; closed Mon (Oct–May)

Phones
The phone numbers given in this book are the local ones, which can be dialled alone for calls made within Monaco. There are no area codes.

Public phones in Monaco require the use of phonecards, which can be purchased in denominations of 50 or 100 units from post offices and *tabacs* (licensed tobacconists, who also sell stamps); most public phones will also accept major credit cards, however.

Post
The central post office is in Monte Carlo, and there are others in La Condamine and Monaco-Ville. Stamps and phonecards can be bought there. Note that only Monaco stamps are valid on mail from

TELEPHONING MONACO

To make calls to Monaco from anywhere else in the world, dial your international access code (usually 00) followed by the international dialling code for Monaco, 377, and then the local Monaco number. Even calls from just across the border in France must start 00 377.

TELEPHONING ABROAD

Calls to abroad (including France) from Monaco begin 00, followed by the country code (France 33, Italy 39, UK 44, Republic of Ireland 353, USA and Canada 1, Australia 61, New Zealand 64, South Africa 27) and then the area code (leaving out the first 0 if there is one) and the number.

the Principality and that they cannot be used on mail posted in France. In all other respects the efficient Monégasque postal service is integrated with the French La Poste; postcards to the UK and Ireland will normally arrive in two–three days, taking a little longer to non-European destinations.

Central Post Office ⓐ Palais de la Scala, 1 av Henri-Dunant ☎ 3631 🕐 08.00–19.00 Mon–Fri, 08.00–12.00 Sat

ELECTRICITY

Monaco runs on 220 v with two-pin plugs. British appliances will need a simple adaptor, obtainable in the UK or at any electrical or hardware store in Monaco. American and other equipment designed for 110 v will need a transformer (*transformateur*), easily acquired locally if you can't buy one at home.

TRAVELLERS WITH DISABILITIES

Monaco's layout on a steep hillside doesn't make it the best of destinations for visitors with impaired mobility, and the buses are not adapted for wheelchairs. On the other hand, the generous provision of lifts and moving walkways around town does make sightseeing easier than it would otherwise be for visitors in wheelchairs and their companions. The period around the Grand Prix race (see page 12) is especially unsuitable, owing to the many safety barriers and fences erected in streets around the course. Many of the hotels have made provision for guests with mobility problems, as have the Collection des Voitures Anciennes (see page 105), the Musée Océanographique (page 84) and the Casino (page 64). The Jardin Exotique is virtually impossible for wheelchairs but most of the other parks are manageable. One car-hire company can rent out Peugeot 309 cars equipped for wheelchairs: **Hertz Monaco** ⓐ 27 blvd Albert 1er, at the Ste-Dévote car park ⓣ 93 50 79 60 ⓛ 08.30–19.00 Mon–Fri, 08.30–12.30 Sat, 08.30–13.00 Sun ⓦ www.hertz.fr

Useful organisations for advice and information include:

Association Monégasque des Handicapés Moteurs (Monaco Association for the Mobility Disabled) This has a survey of facilities for disabled people in the Principality. ⓐ 9 rue Princesse Marie de Lorraine ⓣ 93 50 71 00

Handiplage/Audioplage This organisation, based on the right-hand side of the central jetty on Larvotto beach, offers the blind and people with reduced mobility the opportunity to enjoy the pleasures of swimming. They have amphibious chairs, toilets, showers and adapted parking facilities. ⓐ Plage de Larvotto ⓣ 06 78 63 09 41 ⓛ 10.00–17.00 daily (July–mid-Sept)

⬤ *An aerial view of the Principality*

RADAR This is the principal UK forum and pressure group for people with disabilities. ❷ 12 City Forum, 250 City Road, London EC1V 8AF ❶ (020) 7250 3222 Ⓦ www.radar.org.uk

SATH (Society for Accessible Travel & Hospitality) This organisation advises US-based travellers with disabilities. ❷ 347 Fifth Ave, Suite 610, New York, NY 10016 ❶ (212) 447 7284 Ⓦ www.sath.org

TOURIST INFORMATION

The main tourist office is in the centre of Monte Carlo, at the opposite end of the Jardins de la Petite Afrique park from the Café de Paris. It stocks a wide range of literature and maps and has helpful staff who are happy to make accommodation bookings and sell tickets for many attractions and events. The office's website gives a very good overview of Monaco's attractions, events and practical information for visitors. There are also information kiosks in the summer (mid-June–Sept) at the old rail station in La Condamine, on Quai Albert 1er at the main harbour, on the roof of the main old town car park (Parking des Pêcheurs) and in the Jardin Exotique. Two other information kiosks are open all year round; these can be found at the railway station and Nice airport.

Direction du Tourisme et des Congrès de la Principauté de Monaco

ⓐ 2a blvd des Moulins, Monte Carlo ❶ 92 16 61 16 Ⓦ www.visit monaco.com Ⓛ 09.00–19.00 Mon–Sat, 10.00–12.00 Sun

Websites

In addition to the official tourist office websites, the following sites are useful for planning your trip:

Mairie de Monaco The city council's website is particularly informative on municipally administered parks, attractions and events.
Ⓦ www.monaco-mairie.mc

Monte Carlo Online The English may be a little quaint, but there's a lot of useful information on the site's listings search engine.
Ⓦ www.monte-carlo.mc

Sites covering the entire Riviera include Ⓦ www.cotedazur-tourisme.com (the official tourism site of the French Riviera) Ⓦ www.cotedazur-en-fetes.com (covering events on the Riviera) and Ⓦ http://riviera.angloinfo.com (offering English-speaking services and information)

Yellow Pages

If you're trying to track down or contact a business of any sort, the France and Monaco online Yellow Pages directories are very useful.
Ⓦ (France) www.pagesjaunes.fr; (Monaco) www.pagesjaunes monaco.com

Listings & brochures

The Monaco tourist office (see opposite) publishes a range of listings and brochures to enhance your stay in Monaco, in particular *Bienvenue*, a monthly list of events combined with an at-a-glance guide to practical information of all kinds. For in-depth shopping and dining details, have a look at its annual publication *Monaco Shopping*. Their little booklet *Monaco Loisirs* is also worth picking up; it contains not only a city map and a bus map but also tear-out discount vouchers for just about every attraction in the Principality that charges for admission.

Emergencies

EMERGENCY NUMBERS
Police ❶ 17 (❶ if calling from a mobile phone ❶ 112)
Ambulance/Fire service ❶ 18 or 93 30 19 45
Night pharmacy or doctor on duty ❶ 141
(if calling from a public phone ❶ 93 25 33 25)
Hospital emergency ❶ 97 98 97 69

MEDICAL SERVICES
Centre Hospitalier Princesse Grace Main hospital, with 24-hour
emergency service. ❸ Av Pasteur ❶ 97 98 99 00 ⓦ www.chpg.mc
Riviera Medical Services English-speaking doctors on call
(not necessarily for emergencies) ❶ 00 33 4 93 26 12 70

⬤ *If you lose something, make straight for the police station*

> **EMERGENCY PHRASES**
>
> | **Help!** | **Fire!** | **Stop!** |
> |---|---|---|
> | Au secours! | Au feu! | Stop! |
> | *Ohsercoor!* | *Oh fur!* | *Stop!* |
>
> **Call an ambulance/a doctor/the police/the fire service!**
> Appelez une ambulance/un médecin/la police/les pompiers!
> *Ahperleh ewn ombewlongss/ahng mehdsang/lah poleess/
> leh pompeeyeh!*

POLICE

For general police assistance, contact the Sureté Publique (see page 146). To report or recover lost property, call ☎ 93 15 30 18.

EMBASSIES & CONSULATES

Addresses are for Monaco itself unless otherwise stated. The phone numbers given are those for calling from Monaco.

Australia Embassy ④ 4 rue Jean Rey, Paris, France ☎ 00 33 1 40 59 33 00

Canada Hon Consul ④ 1 av Henry Dunant ☎ 97 70 62 42

New Zealand Embassy ④ 7 rue Léonard da Vinci, Paris, France
☎ 00 33 1 45 01 43 43

Republic of Ireland Consulate ④ 5 av des Citronniers ☎ 93 15 70 00

South Africa Hon Consul General ④ 26 bis blvd Princesse Charlotte
☎ 93 25 24 26

UK Hon Consul ④ 11 av St Michel ☎ 93 50 99 54

USA Consulate ④ 7 av Gustave V, 3rd Floor, Nice, France
☎ 00 33 4 93 88 89 55

ACKNOWLEDGEMENTS

Thomas Cook Publishing wishes to thank ETHEL DAVIES, to whom the copyright belongs, for the photographs in this book, except for the following images:

Dreamstime, pages 5 (Alexskopje), 104 (Amaranta), 109 (Manwolste), 119 (Dimitrisurkov); iStockphoto, pages 7 (Holger Mette), 15 (Veniamin Kraskov), 81 (Kevin Tietz), 145 (stocknshares); Rob Lee, page 32; Monaco Tourisme, pages 19 & 151; SBM Monte Carlo, page 13; Asja Sirova/BigStockPhoto.com, page 49; Stockphoto.com, pages 42–3 (Cornel Stefan Achirei), 137 (Specular Photo); Craig Toron/SXC.hu, page 38.

For CAMBRIDGE PUBLISHING MANAGEMENT LIMITED:
Project editor: Ed Robinson
Layout: Paul Queripel
Proofreaders: Kate Taylor & Tom Lee

Send your thoughts to
books@thomascook.com

- **Found a great bar, club, shop or must-see sight that we don't feature?**
- **Like to tip us off about any information that needs a little updating?**
- **Want to tell us what you love about this handy little guidebook and more importantly how we can make it even handier?**

Then here's your chance to tell all! Send us ideas, discoveries and recommendations today and then look out for your valuable input in the next edition of this title.

Email the above address (stating the title) or write to:
pocket guides Series Editor, Thomas Cook Publishing, PO Box 227, Coningsby Road, Peterborough PE3 8SB, UK.

WHAT'S IN YOUR GUIDEBOOK?

Independent authors Impartial up-to-date information from our travel experts who meticulously source local knowledge.

Experience Thomas Cook's 165 years in the travel industry and guidebook publishing enriches every word with expertise you can trust.

Travel know-how Thomas Cook has thousands of staff working around the globe, all living and breathing travel.

Editors Travel-publishing professionals, pulling everything together to craft a perfect blend of words, pictures, maps and design.

You, the traveller We deliver a practical, no-nonsense approach to information, geared to how you really use it.

Useful phrases

English	French	Approx pronunciation
BASICS		
Yes	Oui	*Wee*
No	Non	*Nong*
Please	S'il vous plaît	*Silvoo play*
Thank you	Merci	*Mehrsee*
Hello	Bonjour	*Bongzhoor*
Goodbye	Au revoir	*Oh revwahr*
Excuse me	Excusez-moi	*Ekskewzeh-mwah*
Sorry	Désolé(e)	*Dehzoleh*
That's okay	Ça va	*Sa va*
I don't speak French	Je ne parle pas français	*Zher ner pahrl pah frongsay*
Do you speak English?	Parlez-vous anglais?	*Pahrlay-voo onglay?*
Good morning	Bonjour	*Bongzhoor*
Good afternoon	Bonjour	*Bongzhoor*
Good evening	Bonsoir	*Bongswah*
Goodnight	Bonne nuit	*Bun nwee*
My name is ...	Je m'appelle ...	*Zher mahpehl ...*
NUMBERS		
One	Un/Une	*Ahng/Oon*
Two	Deux	*Dur*
Three	Trois	*Trwah*
Four	Quatre	*Kahtr*
Five	Cinq	*Sank*
Six	Six	*Seess*
Seven	Sept	*Seht*
Eight	Huit	*Weet*
Nine	Neuf	*Nurf*
Ten	Dix	*Deess*
Twenty	Vingt	*Vang*
Fifty	Cinquante	*Sangkohnt*
One hundred	Cent	*Sohn*
SIGNS & NOTICES		
Airport	Aéroport	*Ah-ehrohpohr*
Rail station	Gare	*Gahr*
Platform	Quai	*Kay*
Smoking/ No smoking	Permit de fumer/ Interdit de fumer	*Permee der foomeh/ Anterdee der foomeh*
Toilets	Toilettes	*Twahlet*
Ladies/Gentlemen	Femmes/Hommes	*Fam/Om*
Bus	Bus	*Booss*